Being a Successful Interpreter

D1523235

Being a Successful Interpreter: Adding value and delivering excellence is a practice-oriented guide to the future of interpreting and the ways in which interpreters can adjust their business and professional practices for the changing market.

The book considers how globalisation and human migration have brought interpreting to the forefront and the subsequent need for interpreters to serve a more diverse client base in more varied contexts. At its core is the view that interpreters must move from the traditional impartial and distant approach to become committed to adding value for their clients.

Features include:

- interviews with leading interpreting experts such as Valeria Aliperta, Judy and Dagmar Jenner, and Esther Navarro-Hall
- examples from authentic interpreting practice
- practice-driven, research-backed discussion of the challenges facing the future of interpreting
- guides for personal development
- ideas for group and development activities within professional associations
- additional resources available on the Routledge Translation Studies Portal at: http://cw.routledge.com/textbooks/translationstudies/.

Being a Successful Interpreter is a practical and thorough guide to the business and personal aspects of interpreting. Written in an engaging and user-friendly manner, it is ideal for professional interpreters practising in conference, medical, court, business, and public service settings, as well as for students and recent graduates of interpreting studies.

Jonathan Downie is a French–English and English–French conference interpreter as well as a researcher, writer, and speaker in interpreting and translation. His doctoral thesis at Heriot-Watt University focused on expectations of interpreters in church settings, which started him on the idea of using research to help interpreters. He regularly writes on the connections between research and practice in translation and interpreting for the *ITI Bulletin* and *VKD Kurier*.

Being a Successful Interpreter

Interpreter

Adding value and delivering excellence

Jonathan Downie

Routledge
Taylor & Francis Group

LONDON AND NEW YORK

First published 2016
by Routledge
2 Park Square, Milton Park, Abingdon, Oxon OX14 4RN

and by Routledge
711 Third Avenue, New York, NY 10017

Routledge is an imprint of the Taylor & Francis Group, an informa business

© 2016 Jonathan Downie

The right of Jonathan Downie to be identified as author of this work has been asserted by him in accordance with sections 77 and 78 of the Copyright, Designs and Patents Act 1988.

British Library Cataloguing-in-Publication Data
A catalogue record for this book is available from the British Library

Library of Congress Cataloging-in-Publication Data
Names: Downie, Jonathan, author.
Title: Being a successful interpreter : adding value and delivering excellence / Jonathan Downie
Description: Milton Park, Abingdon, Oxon ; New York : Routledge, New York, [2016] | Includes bibliographical references and index.
Identifiers: LCCN 2015041041| ISBN 9781138119680 (hbk : alk. paper) | ISBN 9781138119697 (pbk : alk. paper) | ISBN 9781315652191 (ebk)
Subjects: LCSH: Translating and interpreting--Handbooks, manuals, etc. | Translating services.
Classification: LCC P306.2 .D69 2016 | DDC 418/.02--dc23
LC record available at http://lccn.loc.gov/2015041041

ISBN: 978-1-138-11968-0 (hbk)
ISBN: 978-1-138-11969-7 (pbk)
ISBN: 978-1-315-65219-1 (ebk)

Typeset in Times New Roman and Gill Sans
by Bookbright Media

Contents

Interpreting at a crossroads

Suddenly, things don't seem as stable as they used to be for interpreting. In the United Kingdom, rates for court interpreting have tumbled to the point where more than 80 per cent of professional interpreters refused to work under a new contract when it was brought into place in 2011[1]. The largely unregulated nature of freelance interpreting means that interpreters all over the world need to carefully select the clients with whom they work to avoid poor conditions and late payment or even no payment at all. Add to that the rise of machine interpreting in the guise of Skype Translator[2] and moves by Google to integrate Google Translate into an automatic interpreting platform[3], and it seems like there is pressure on all sides of the profession.

Against this background, it may be surprising that interpreting is by no means on its last legs. Social media has proven a boon, with the '#1nt' hashtag becoming a common sight on Twitter and Facebook groups on various aspects of interpreting, from training and note-taking to research and networking. It is becoming increasingly easier to find books, training materials, and even courses on interpreting. Interpreters are fast moving from being a rare and rarefied elite to becoming a mutually supportive group of professionals with contacts all over the world.

Today, professional interpreters stand at a crossroads. Behind them, the well-worn paths to professionalism and even regular work seem to be showing signs of wear and tear. Does it really make sense to talk about neutrality and the simple passing on of information when successful medical treatment might depend on doctors being helped to grasp the cultural chasm that separates them from their patients who speak other languages? As technology shrinks the world, is it still valid to argue that interpreters will only perform at their best if present in the room with their clients and surrounded by expensive and cumbersome booths and transmitters?

In front of us looms the challenge of balancing our understandable desire to carry the torch of excellence with a need to take into account how the world has fundamentally changed since our profession was born. Whether you trace professional interpreting to Ancient Egypt, Paris, or Nuremberg, the fact is that multilingual communication is no longer the sole preserve of the conquering monarch, travelling diplomat, or passionate missionary. In fact, it is hard to find an area of life that doesn't involve interpreters. Business deals, trade negotiations, hiring, firing, treating, counselling, judging, competing, presenting, press relations, networking, and even dating can be and are done with the help of interpreters. Wherever we look, there we are.

This book aims to help us meet that challenge. At its core is the simple idea that the future of interpreting must be different simply because the world in which we interpret has changed and is changing still. Some people reading this need only take a look at the device in their hands: a sleek electronic gadget that allows you to read books without ever turning a physical page or walking into a bookshop, to understand the reality of those changes. So, instead of concentrating on the minutiae of our language processing or the detail of our contracts, I want to take a slightly wider view. The aim of this book is to help us do two things: add value to our clients and add value to our profession.

Concentrating on these two things might explain the reasons why I choose not to cover some subjects. Rates, conditions, and national contracts, as important as they are, are not subjects I will delve into. The reason for this is simple: as much as we all love to debate these matters, they are purely indicators of much bigger processes. Take rates, for example. Whether your preference is the AIIC standard, or a local recommendation, day rates or hourly fees, the amount that you make at the end of each job simply indicates how valuable the client felt you were to them. Businesses always find room in their budgets for priorities. If money for interpreting seems tight or even non-existent, that tells us that interpreting is not seen as valuable, and no amount of rate campaigning or attempts at collective bargaining will change that.

The same can be said for national contracts. As galling as it is to see interpreting rates tumble to unacceptable levels, we will gain much more leverage by working to change the attitudes that make interpreting seem like a waste of time than we will by camping outside government offices. Money is always found for priorities. The key then is to show how interpreting is and should be a priority.

Now I realise that those last two paragraphs might be upsetting for some. I am not saying that it is okay to undervalue interpreting, nor am I saying that we should blithely accept reductions in pay and conditions. What I am saying is that we need to understand that the topics that often take up so much of our time need to be understood in their proper contexts. As translators have found out, work on increasing your value and money takes care of itself. By all means, let's fight to change the conditions under which interpreters are asked to work, but please, let's do so intelligently and with an understanding of what it means to be valued by our clients.

And then there is technology. It seems that no sane interpreter would now leave the house without a tablet computer, a smartphone, and maybe even a smart pen. Each month seems to see the creation or creative use of another piece of technology. Amidst all this, the subject of remote interpreting looms large. Is remote interpreting a wonderful way to reduce our travel costs or is it just one more way for interpreters to be sidelined?

Considering this, I wonder if our horizons have become too small. While we passionately discuss the pros and cons of tablets, remote interpreting, and the like, our clients are getting on with life – running their businesses, delivering babies, presenting cases. I doubt that very many, if any, of our regular clients have opinions on whether we should be there with them or interpreting from our summerhouse in the Bahamas (if only!). What they might well care about is whether our interpreting will do the job they are paying for it to do. Will our interpreting help them argue their cases, sell their widgets, or guide patients through treatment?

In essence, technology should matter to us only to the extent that it helps us add value to our clients. It is also not entirely wrong to measure that added value in terms of the money we can save them. So, if we can find technology that makes interpreting cheaper without compromising the service we deliver, it makes sense to use it. On the other hand, if using a smart pen, smartphone, and glossary app won't make much difference, we can feel free to leave them at home.

The reason why technology doesn't have its own chapter in the book then is very similar to the reason why I don't delve into the ins and outs of rates and contracts. While rates and contracts are reflections of the value our clients think we add, the technology we use is simply a way of helping us deliver more value. In other words, what we do with the technology is far more important than the technology itself. Value added, not gadgetry, is the key.

Value is what this book is about. The future of interpreting is found in the value produced by interpreters. Put another way, I want to focus on the things that will lead us to better relationships with our clients, better pay, and more helpful conditions rather than on any of those individual issues. From understanding how to hone our skills with daily practice to keeping ourselves mentally and physically healthy, this book will cover ten key challenges that we all need to meet, whether we are sign-language interpreters working in primary education or conference interpreters working in the highest echelons of political power.

As well as being based on the idea that we need to concentrate on producing value, this book is based on one more foundational thought: meeting the challenges of the future of interpreting means working both as individuals and as teams. That might seem pretty basic, but it goes straight to the heart of what it means to be a professional interpreter.

To be a professional interpreter means *being an interpreter*. It means that each of us individually needs to have the skills, attitudes, and knowledge required to deliver the assignments we get with excellence. If we stop getting work because we are not delivering quality and value, that is an individual problem. No professional association, lobbying group, or union will ever be able to force clients to work with incompetent interpreters and neither should they. To some extent then, our success depends on our individual competence. We are each responsible for our own quality and for the value we deliver as interpreters.

To be a professional interpreter also means *being a professional*. It means that we form part of a great, if sometimes less than coherent, community of practice[4].

We are responsible to demonstrate to each of our clients what it means to be a professional and to learn (and modify) what this means alongside other interpreters. There is no such thing as a one-person Community of Practice. We grow and develop and learn together. To be a professional interpreter means that you join the family of other interpreters, wherever they work, whomever they work for. That means that some things need to be changed by groups, such as professional associations, campaign groups, and PR teams. While we are each responsible to join and reflect the values of the interpreting community, the community needs to work as a unit to help bring about precisely the kinds of changes in how interpreting is valued that I outlined above.

To be a freelance professional interpreter means *being a business*. We need to get a handle on the fact that, as freelancers, we are businesspeople. Here our siblings in translation are way ahead of us. It only takes a few minutes of intelligent web searching to find volumes for translators on how to market your services, gain better clients, become a brand, and so on. As interpreters, we often want to pretend that we don't need to know these things. It is still rare to see a webinar or training course about the business side of our profession.

That attitude is changing. Our pricing structure, clientele, and balance sheet are the result of our choices. Yes, there are inequalities. Yes, some things are unfair, but there is always something we can do as businesspeople to create value wherever we are.

We all know that, for some interpreters, national contracts and shrinking government budgets limit freedom of manoeuvre. If you are a sign-language interpreter or a medical interpreter, you can create all the value you like, but it seems that rates will always be controlled by an outside entity. What seems to be needed in such situations is an intelligent look at what other income streams might be possible and even, depending on your language pairing, whether a different client mix might be needed.

Of course, all this is complex. When many of the users of your services are people who have been historically subject to discrimination, it would be unethical to abandon them in the pursuit of more cash. In situations like these, it would be fair to say that action from the wider community and partnership across forms of interpreting will be needed if anything will change on the ground. It is perfectly ethical, however, to look for income streams to augment your earnings to give you more leeway until change comes.

Where this book aims to help is to put the tools in your hands to accelerate this process. Every chapter aims to make a practical difference in how we interpret, how we market our services, and how we contribute to the future of our profession, with all but one of them being based on solid research by established experts. The only chapter that isn't built on the foundation of research is Chapter 10, which is all about the future of our profession and being pro-active in the ways we look for clients. The reason for that is simple: by definition, no one can research the future. But we can play our part in shaping it.

Structure of this book

To make life easy for busy interpreters, I have split the rest of the book into ten chapters, which can be read in any order, although I would strongly suggest that Chapter 1 is read first, as it forms the cornerstone of the book. Each chapter comes with an interview with a leading expert in that area of interpreting and a guide for both individual and group application.

Chapter 1 begins by discussing the view that it is time we ditched the view of interpreters as impartial language machines once and for all. Instead, I argue on the basis of established research and professional experience that the time has come to sell our work and ourselves in terms of the value that we bring to our clients and the ways that we can partner with them to help their events succeed. The need to understand how this can be done within our ethical duties is covered in detail. There is no one in the world better qualified to be interviewed on this topic than Penny Karanasiou. Penny is not only an experienced conference and business negotiation interpreter but a seasoned businessperson, running Erminia Network of Translators in Greece, a thriving group of translation and interpreting agencies. Penny also happens to be a leading expert in business-negotiation interpreting, giving her powerful insights into how we can add value to clients and their events.

Chapter 2 moves from adding value to clients to adding value to our profession, centring on the subject of initial training, the kind usually offered by universities and colleges. Here I look closely at the role of such training and will examine what it really takes to go from gawking interpreting newbie to established professional. I argue that all of us have a stake in the future of training since the professionals produced will one day be our colleagues. It is therefore in all of our interests to make sure that we help universities and training providers add as much value as possible. At the end of this chapter, I interview Kirsty Heimerl-Moggan, who trains interpreters at two different universities, as well being a high-level interpreter herself and doing a PhD on note taking.

Chapter 3 continues with the subject of training but moves us on the journey from established professional to expert. The big discussion here is the role of continued professional development, especially the role of reflection and time spent working on our domain-specific knowledge. In short, I want to suggest that the only way to ensure we keep offering high-quality interpreting is to make sure we keep our skills, knowledge, and thinking up to date. This chapter ends with an interview with Dr Elisabet Tiselius, a conference interpreter and senior lecturer in Translation and Interpreting Studies at Stockholm University. Her expertise happens to be in how interpreters can become experts in their own right.

Chapter 4 handles the under-discussed subject of branding and PR. The starting point for this chapter is a return to the central argument of this book, which is that rates and conditions are a result of the value clients give to our services, and so it is this value that we need to work on. I look at the way clients might perceive the value of both interpreting as a profession and individual interpreters, alongside some surprising results of our current sales pitches for our profession. This chapter ends with an interview with the *doyenne* of marketing and branding for the language industries: Valeria Aliperta.

Chapter 5 covers the role of professional associations and groups. While most of us started work with the view that the main role of a professional association was to set rates and conditions, this view is being challenged. Social media has encouraged the formation of groups that have neither the political clout nor the financial resources to force clients to do anything. So what are they for and why are they useful? How do they change the role of the long-standing associations? I delve into this and also briefly cover why the success of professional associations should be important to all interpreters and why it makes sense to join one. The interview helps to illuminate the world of established professional associations with a discussion with Iwan Davies, the Chair of the Institute of Translation and Interpreting, one of Europe's leading professional associations.

Chapter 6 maintains the theme and importance of groups, this time covering the need to unite our divided professions. All of us, after all, are professional interpreters, and it is in our interests that our profession is seen as united, valuable, and important. I cover some of the historical reasons for our divisions and some far more important reasons for healing those divisions. This chapter features an interview with Judy and Dagmar Jenner, who are not only the authors of the groundbreaking book *The Entrepreneurial Linguist* but also people whose careers illustrate perfectly what uniting our profession looks like.

Chapter 7 tackles the view that there is interpreting research and interpreting practice and 'never the twain shall meet'. Here the aim is not just to present recent research that practising interpreters need to understand but also to help knock down any perceived walls between the two worlds and show how knowledge of recent research can help us to add value. The interview with Professor Ebru Diriker centres on what this balance of interpreting research and practice looks like in the life of a practitioner-researcher.

Chapter 8 moves from the mind to the body, discussing health, nutrition, and exercise. Here, I investigate subjects such as caffeine, sugar, as well as the healthy habits we need to develop to keep our brains in working order. After all, it's very hard to add value if we are feeling awful. If there is one person who has made a name discussing these subjects, it is conference interpreter Kamil Celoch, and the interview with him focuses on how we can put all this knowledge into practice.

Chapter 9 progresses from how to fill one's belly to how to get belly laughs. I broach the subject of humour, focusing not on how to handle jokes but how to make them. Based on the view that any profession worth doing is worth laughing about, I examine the importance of humour for interpreters who want to consistently add value, and talk about how we can responsibly enjoy a bit of mirth. The interview with interpreter and stand-up comedian Matthew Perret is sure to give you a few giggles, too.

Chapter 10 rounds off the book by setting our sights high. While most of us were schooled to see large international political entities as the greatest places to interpret, I endeavour to imagine a world where interpreting becomes second nature to any growing global organisation. While big international organisations will continue to exert a strong pull, I look at the benefits of spreading our wings. The final interview with Esther Navarro-Hall delves into what it takes to 'make it' amongst direct clients.

Notes

1 www.linguistlounge.org/all-articles/news/776-81-of-court-interpreters-boycott-capita-register.
2 www.skype.com/en/translator-preview.
3 www.bbc.co.uk/news/technology-30812277.
4 A great introduction can be found in Etienne Wenger, 'Communities of Practice: A Brief Introduction', 2011, https://scholarsbank.uoregon.edu/xmlui/handle/1794/11736.

Chapter 1

From neutral conduits to committed partners

Working actively with clients

Chapter summary

This chapter covers:

- What it means to partner with clients,
- Why our traditional values may be working against us and how to replace them,
- The challenge and potential of partnership.

It had been an exhausting few days. I was waiting to conduct the very last interview of my visit to Germany. I had interviewed interpreters, audience members, and speakers, all in an attempt to get a hold of what the people in this particular organisation expected of interpreters. As a card-carrying, Master's-graduate, conference interpreter, I had my own views. Like most interpreters, I was led to believe that we were there to pass on information and, if possible, do so in a way that was pleasant to listen to. What happened next with that information? That was anyone's guess and, frankly, outside our purview.

Here, in an organisation where interpreting was at the core of everything that went on, they had their own views. "I feel like, if there is no interpreter, I am not complete", said one speaker. "The interpreter is not a machine", said an audience member. And then came the most stunning idea of all, in this, my last interview – the speaker told me that he had learned to speak more effectively by working with interpreters. He wanted and even expected that interpreters would let him know when an illustration or idea wouldn't go over well.

The interpreters here were anything but mere 'language service providers'. They were, in a word, *partners*.

When was the last time you felt like a partner on an assignment? Personally, partnership is not something that clients routinely ask for. More usual is a situation such as this: Interpreters get the brief, try to make sense of the brief, do term research, look for videos of the speakers and then make big lists of terminology and names. We arrive on-site, chat to the sound technicians, find sources of caffeine and water, look for the toilets, and settle down to work. We work the shift and swap confused glances with the rest of the team. Did any of us actually fully understand what was going on? Did we know why the audience found the chair's jokes funny? And what was that about the sub-committee of the working party of the study group of the non-executive under-management team on esoteric bureaucracy?

I am exaggerating a little, but I would guess that most interpreters, even the most experienced among us, have had assignments that looked and felt similar. That detached, almost dehumanising type of interpreting is not new, either. Well-known researcher Franz Pöchhacker[1] quoted early conference interpreter Jean Herbert as saying that the interpreter "sits in his glass case, without any contact with the other participants, and translates mechanically what is said on subjects in which he is not interested by people whom he does not know". On the same page, he also quotes an anonymous interpreter interviewed in 1985 who said, "One thing I regret is that the real function of interpreting, that is, building bridges between mentalities, is drowned out by a flood of words and no longer applies. I had assumed, idealistically, that language as a vehicle would lead to better understanding and respect for the mentality of others; but this is possible only in exceptional cases". How many of us feel the same way?

The point of this chapter is absolutely not to hold up one organisation as perfect. What I do want to do, however, is to ask whether the way we currently practise interpreting and work with clients must stay as it is right now.

Before I suggest how interpreters can effectively partner with their clients, let's explore the realities of interpreting as it is currently. I will begin with conference interpreting before expanding the discussion to include interpreting in other settings, something the following interview will take even further.

Firstly, exploring the realities of interpreting starts with this simple question: If I asked you to define 'excellent interpreting', how would you respond?

If you are like most interpreters, and indeed, like many clients, your answer might be as follows:

Interpreting needs to be accurate, use the right terminology, be in well-formed sentences, grammatically correct, and delivered with a pleasant voice. Interpreters should be well prepared and appropriately dressed, be impartial, have excellent memories, and understand the different ways people use language. They should, in fact, be so good that it's as if the source-language speaker suddenly learned a new language. In short, they should be so seamless, it's as if they don't even exist.

That definition is the one that you will find, in one form or another, in professional codes of conduct, university training programs, books, and magazines. And, despite changes in training and years of research, it is still one that appears to be held by most conference interpreters to this day[2]. On those rare occasions when interpreters are interviewed in the media, they will very likely talk about their profession in those kinds of terms[3]. Interpreters discuss, sell, and advertise interpreting in the same terms, even if some of us were trained to think otherwise.

This also occurs in other forms of interpreting. In one study, Dr Robyn Dean wanted to test whether ethical reasoning among sign-language interpreters and those who provide continued professional development (CPD) courses for them had changed over recent years. She decided to attend a webinar on how to apply a code of conduct to everyday work[1]. After reading the materials used to give them ethical training and listening to the ways interpreters were told to solve these dilemmas, she came to the conclusion that not much had changed. Despite everything they might be taught at university, interpreters and some trainers still seem to wander back to the seemingly safe surroundings of neutrality and advertise themselves as mobile dictionaries for hire, even when this means acting in a way that goes against the interests of their clients.

It does seem that clients might favour the very kind of neutral, invisible interpreting I am trying to argue against in this chapter. In the vast majority of studies of client expectations, the same key criteria come up again and again: fidelity to the original, correct use of terminology, and logical cohesion. Clients also regularly express the view that interpreters should stay in the background and be as invisible as possible[5].

So, do we and our clients know exactly what interpreting is about? Will accuracy, impartiality, and invisibility will bring lots of well-paying, happy, repeat clients?

It's not that simple. Dig beneath the surface of these seemingly straightforward expectations and something confusing happens. Take the work of Turkish interpreter Şeyda Eraslan[6].

She surveyed clients at a teacher training seminar in Turkey. When she asked them questions that covered much the same ground as my definition, the clients all responded positively. They wanted accurate, neutral, nice-sounding interpreters. Once she started asking more specific questions, however, such as whether consecutive interpreters should interrupt the speaker for clarifications, or whether they should explain culture-specific references, their answers were different. Suddenly, they weren't so interested in nice, invisible interpreting any more. What they wanted were interpreters who worked with the speakers and the audience to ensure the event was successful.

Here we have a clear conflict. Talk to clients about 'interpreting' and they seem to want what basically amounts to dictionaries on legs. Talk to them about their specific event or situation and they start talking an entirely different language altogether. Suddenly, interpreting becomes much more about enabling communication and perhaps even improving it. In short, they want interpreters who act as if they want the event to succeed.

This idea of interpreters working for the success of the event might just be what we need to reverse a rather disturbing trend. It's no secret that some clients are now actively looking for ways to get around paying for professionals. Governments are reducing the requirements for working in courts and hospitals, major companies are seeing how far they can get by with the work of their own staff, and TV stations are relying on their presenters over professionals who would love the opportunity.

It is very easy and almost accurate to blame these trends on the never-ending quest to trim budgets. In most developed economies, interpreting is still classed as a 'cost item'. Couple this with the suspicion that an interpreter can simply be anyone who has a decent level of language skills, or that all you need to do the job is the right software and a decent microphone and you can understand why we aren't always valued.

Very few professional interpreters would follow such simplified logic. Most would argue that there is something that you can get from a professional that untrained interpreters simply can't provide. But what is that 'something'? To be honest, many of the views of interpreting still apparent in our professions can't really give you an answer. After all, if interpreters are happy to describe themselves as impartial, strictly accurate masters of terminology then they are pretty much selling themselves as walking dictionaries anyway. It is ironic then that interpreters become frustrated with clients who replace them with bilingual staff or software.

In reflecting on these considerations, I think that blaming budget cuts for the use of untrained interpreters is only a partial answer to the question. As I said in the Introduction, businesses always find room in the budget for priorities. So why isn't professional interpreting seen as a priority in many places?

The answer is surprisingly simple: people fail to see the value added by professional interpreting. The 'something' that clients are looking for is that ability to make the event or report or consultation better or more effective than it would have been otherwise. While it is becoming increasingly easier to persuade people that reaching out to those who speak other languages will have concrete benefits, there are still fights to be won to convince them that professional interpreters are the people to make that happen.

For example, take the case of TV reporting: TV channels are not exactly short of cash when it comes to hiring presenters, purchasing equipment, and organising outdoor broadcasts. They think nothing of sending expensive staff halfway across the world to cover a few games of football, but will baulk at the idea of sending professional interpreters with them. According to María Gracia Torres Díaz and Allesandro Ghignoli from Malaga University in Spain[7], one particular Spanish sports channel has not only used their presenters as interpreters but has even argued that they did a better job than the professionals they used to hire.

The station argued that, while the professionals are really good at being accurate, what they lack is the flair for producing TV-ready content and soundbites. Unsurprisingly, they contended that their journalists, for whom soundbites come naturally, deliver that side of the job with flair.

I imagine most interpreters would be scandalised at such claims and want to start some kind of letter-writing campaign. Diaz and Ghignoli took what I think is a much more helpful approach. They decided to put those claims to the test. They lined up some of their top interpreting students and pitted them against some bilingual trainee journalists. They asked both groups to interpret the same short text from an interview with a professional motorcycle racer.

The results were rather embarrassing, really. It turns out that the TV channel people were right. The student interpreters were accurate but didn't come across as engaging. The journalists might have left out some information but delivered much smoother journalistic content. They also put their sports knowledge to good use, making smart decisions about what people needed to hear and what could be dropped. In short, they added value by putting the needs of the program above any other concerns.

We can make the argument that there are differences between students and professionals, and it might be possible that professional interpreters would deliver perfect content every time. If we believe that, however, we have to either believe that the particular TV channel somehow managed to get all the bad interpreters or that they are telling half-truths. Neither is a good basis on which to start a conversation about changing their minds.

If the TV executives are right then the responsibility falls squarely on the heads of interpreters. If at least part of the problem with interpreting is that it doesn't always correspond to what clients want or need, then it is the job of the interpreter to remedy that. In short, if interpreters are not delivering what clients really want then they need to change their approach.

When it comes to changing one's approach, it helps to turn to our pyjama-wearing, CAT-tool using, detail-minded colleagues: translators. Over the past two or three years, it has become far more common for translators to publicly talk about their quest to deliver translations that do specific jobs. We have tourism translators who want to deliver texts that attract tourists, finance translators who want to write annual reports that are clear and send the right message, and technical translators who make usable manuals. In fact, saying that translations are supposed to do something useful for both the client and the end user is now taken as stating the obvious.

Apply this to interpreting and our traditional values become less attractive. What if, instead of making perfect accuracy and impartiality non-negotiable, we make it our goal to work with our clients to deliver an event that fulfils its purpose? What if we made it our goal to help deliver medical consultations where people got superb treatment, PR events that sent people home happy and enthused, court hearings where justice was done, and conferences where people were informed, inspired, and felt at home?

All this means that we have to take on much more responsibility than we are used to. Suddenly, getting access to the agenda becomes less about terminology preparation and more about understanding what will go on and how we can and should help. If we are there to be partners and help the event work, we have to know not just what people are saying but why they are saying it and what they are hoping to achieve. In fact, we might just need to step into their shoes.

The leap from language service provider to committed partner is therefore not a quick or easy one. It is a long, challenging journey that requires all the determination and courage it took to get into the profession, and lots more besides. Foremost among these challenges will be rethinking what we call 'ethics'.

Almost since interpreting was born, it has been thought that neutrality was the most ethical way to work. Interpreters believed that it was only by remaining strictly neutral could they ensure that their considerable power was not being misused. Early interpreters, it seems, realised that they were and are linguistic 'superheroes'. Their superpower is to allow people to communicate across language barriers. They receive the trust of their clients and dare not abuse that trust.

What is the trust based on? If it is based on the idea that interpreters will never omit anything, never make a mistake, and never feel more connected to one 'side' more than another, then all interpreters are unethical. Whatever form of interpreting you look at will involve interpreters making split-second decisions that involve precisely those strategies that we feel uncomfortable to mention. Court interpreters change language registers, conference interpreters omit figures or re-phrase ideas, medical interpreters explain pain scales, church interpreters attenuate offensive content. If our ethics is based on never being involved and never making an obvious difference, then we breach our code of ethics simply by being present in the room.

It's is incredibly uncomfortable to realise that we are, after all, human beings. We have limited brain capacity and must decide what parts of what people said are the most important. Sometimes we might even realise that *how* things are said is equally, if not more, important than the words that came out of the person's mouth.

What should the ethics of interpreting be based on then? At their heart, they should be rooted in the power interpreters wield. When an interpreter steps into the booth or the courtroom or the medical practice, he or she is the most powerful person in the room. Justice cannot be done, diseases cannot be treated, and information cannot be passed adequately without the interpreter. This power should be wielded wisely.

Added to that is the power differential that often arises when two people communicate with the help of an interpreter. Immigrants being interviewed by the police know nothing of what awaits them and can easily be mistreated. Suppliers trading in a new country can easily be hoodwinked by businesses that are already there. Interpreters have to decide how much of their power can and should be used to level that playing field. Is it fair to the paying clients if the interpreter actively prevents them from using their power to get a better deal, even if they do that by deceit? Is it fair to warn the witness, even subtly, that the prosecution is attempting to trap them?

Despite what you might have been taught, there are no easy answers. Our ethics then need to be as much about the process behind our decisions as it is about the decisions themselves. We also need to be aware of another aspect of our work: trust. Clients need to be able to trust that, as far as it depends on us, we will do what we say and say what we do. They need to trust that we will declare any interests that we have and that we will be clear, as much as we can be, as to whose interests we are serving.

This is what my PhD supervisor, Graham Turner, calls "real interpreting"[8] – interpreting which doesn't pretend that it doesn't exist or that it doesn't make a difference but which instead creates an honest, knowing, realistic relationship between interpreters and clients. The basis of this is the fact that no matter how good the interpreter, it will never be feasible or reasonable to pretend that somehow we or they can produce a setup that is identical to the way it would be if everyone spoke the same language. Rather than attempt to hide ourselves in the background, this view of interpreting puts front and centre our role as those who are actively helping clients do their work and achieve their goals.

Trust, then, is not about always trying to establish a middle ground but simply about being clear and honest. The tradition of having a five-minute chat before the start of every job is therefore definitely worth keeping. How else can we help clients understand what interpreting is really about and how limiting and yet empowering it can be? But, of course, such chats also have to involve admission that perfection is not going to happen. Trust necessarily involves helping people understand how we can work most effectively with them and they with us. It is in their interest after all.

If all this sounds like hard work, it's because it is indeed hard work. If it seems like there are still big questions to answer, that's because there are. Every job will require deep thought and preparation that goes far beyond having nice glossaries and shiny technology. If we are going to work as partners and add value to clients, we are the ones who will have to put in most of the work on the front end, at least for the foreseeable future.

The need for deep thought and preparation only increases in situations where it is difficult to decide who exactly your 'client' is. If you are working for an agency on a project that aims to provide a service to a minority community but is paid for by a government department, then it becomes far more difficult to imagine what 'partnership' might mean. Yet, even in these complex, sometimes confusing, jobs there is usually some shared goal or some declared aim that can help ground your work.

There might be five groups of people who all think you should be furthering their aims but the more we research and ask good questions, the greater the chance we have of getting to the point. Closely examining any paperwork and publicity around the event, studying all the details you can, and getting to know the setting and people involved all help put you in the position to deliver the levels of service and attention that everyone needs.

For some time now, interpreters who use dialogue interpreting have had to learn how to read situations. It is now almost a given that knowing you are going to a doctor's appointment or job interview isn't enough. Good interpreting teachers will help you learn to read gestures, language registers, expressions, and the like to help you get to the point of understanding exactly what is going on and how you might want to adjust your performance.

Let me illustrate this with a true story from my career. I was interpreting at an event for people in a wood-related industry. The event lasted a day or so, and included *chuchotage* at an annual general meeting (AGM) and then at a conference. The AGM was challenging. I missed the nuances of what was said and felt completely out of the loop, simply because I didn't know enough about the organisation to interpret intelligently. The concerned look on the faces of the French delegation told me all I needed to know. I had been linguistically accurate but hadn't caught what was meant. "You might struggle tomorrow," said one frowning client. "It will be more technical".

What happened the next day will stick in my memory for a long time. I got through the introductory speeches without much trouble. The first plenary passed by with no real difficulties of note. Then came the 'economic outlook' presented by a respected economist with eons of experience in the wood industries and a PowerPoint presentation that came complete with at least four charts per slide.

Within about thirty seconds I understood what was going on. The entire conference hinged on people understanding their industry's current economic context. The purpose of the talk was to help people become aware of this context and use key economic data in their decision-making processes. Once I realised that, I knew what I had to do. There was simply no way I could give every single data point, but I could make sure I got the trends right and give the same air of breezy confidence that the speaker was excelling at presenting.

Just over halfway through the speech, the head of the French delegation leans behind me and whispers to his colleague, "*Il est bon, cet interprète, n'est-ce pas*" [this interpreter is good, isn't he]. That little sentence made my day. I might not have given every number but I did help make the event a success. The delegation got exactly what they came for and my paying clients got a happy audience. Offers of future work underlined what kind of job I had done. There was no need to persuade these clients that professionals are always best.

Who was I partnering with? To whom was I adding value? A good case could be made for any answer. You could say the speaker received added value, as someone cared enough to make sure his message was received and understood, even at the cost of strict accuracy. You could argue that the members of the French delegation received added value, as someone thought about what their needs actually were and worked to fulfil them. You could also say that the agency and the organisation who commissioned the interpreting received added value, as the delegates went home happy. Not all cases are as clear-cut and it won't always be possible to send everyone home with a smile, but the foundational principle is still the same.

How many of us are used to this kind of deep, reasoned decision making? How many of us are happy to take our share of the responsibility for the success of an event? Those are good questions and ones that, as yet, have no clear answers. Yet, one thing seems to be certain: we can no longer take it for granted that providing accurate interpreting with nice intonation and precise terminology will be enough. It does seem that we have to take seriously the word 'service' in the wonderfully fashionable phrase, 'language service provider'. In fact, perhaps it's time we became partners with our clients, as tricky and messy and challenging as that might be.

Partnership in the success of your clients will always be the best way to persuade them to hire you again. The future of interpreting is in making sure that clients see professional interpreters as partners instead of language machines.

As I mentioned in the Introduction, few people are in a better position to explain to us how that is possible than interpreter, researcher, and successful translation and interpreting entrepreneur, Penny Karanasiou. It is my pleasure to present the first ten-question interview with her.

Interview with Penny Karanasiou

Penny, I know that you have recently undertaken research in business-negotiation interpreting. Could you describe your project and how your findings might help business-negotiation interpreters add value to their clients?

My PhD thesis was on the role of interpreters as perceived and as needed in business-negotiation settings. Through my research, I looked at the perceptions that interpreters have of their role while working in business-negotiation settings, but I also looked at the experiences with and the needs that businesspeople have of interpreters in that setting. What stuck out from my findings was that interpreters seem to define their role within their own bubble, without looking at the needs of clients or of the settings that they are working in. We have to remember that interpreting is a service-provision profession, and as all other service professions look at the end-users' needs, we interpreters ought to do the same. We need to look at the needs of the specific setting, and then define our role or contribution accordingly. We would never think, for instance, that a police officer or a teacher or any other service professional should offer their services without first evaluating the needs of the end-users. Why do interpreters do that? One of my aims undertaking this research project was to change the interpreter's perception of how to perceive their role. I believe it's about time interpreters stopped defining their role within their own bubble or comfort zone and evaluate the needs of the clients, as well as the needs of the specific setting or event.

And could you describe what led you to undertake that research?

I have been working as a business-negotiation interpreter for years. Early in my career I realised that language was not the primary reason that clients preferred to hire me instead of other interpreters in the market. I also realised that what I have learned during my T & I studies was not directly applicable for this setting of work. Therefore, I believed that through my PhD research, I could unfold these issues and contribute something to the field.

What do you think makes business-negotiation interpreting different from, say, court interpreting or medical interpreting?

There are many similarities but also many differences among these settings. Every setting presents different challenges to the interpreters. In court, for example, interpreters' primary stated aim is to convey what is being said in the most 'accurate' way. In business negotiations, though, the main aim is to ensure that the negotiation meeting proceeds and moves forward into a healthy cooperation. Therefore, unintentional *faux pas* or mistakes made due to cultural unawareness can be avoided with the help of an interpreter. Moreover, any issues left unclear can be clarified by the interpreter, or with the help of the interpreter. An interpreter in business meetings is present in order to assist the communication process. The interpreter – as the only person with knowledge of both languages, cultures, ethics, etc. – can help negotiators by explaining or exemplifying all aspects of communication, both verbal and nonverbal.

How would you describe a typical business-negotiation interpreting assignment? What do you do to add value to your clients?

A typical business-negotiation assignment is a roller coaster of emotions and tactics. That is what makes it so interesting and challenging for the interpreter. A business meeting can take place in various settings, like in a meeting room, over dinner, in a showroom, and many more places, and the feelings, emotions, and beliefs are bound to be fluctuating from very positive to very negative. The dynamics of a negotiation meeting are constantly changing.

To add value to my client in those settings, I try to learn my client's aims, budgets, and tactics before entering the negotiation room. In that way, my demeanour would be aligned in the negotiation room with the strategy of the company that has employed me. In the actual negotiation, I'll try to assist the communication process in various ways, even if that means exceeding my 'traditional' interpreter role. For example, since every country has its own protocols and processes of doing things, I explain these protocols and processes to my client if needed, so that he or she does not waste time asking questions to the other parties or even questioning the different processes that one encounters. By informing the clients, I also protect the integrity of the meeting, since negotiators are better prepared for diversity.

In addition to being an interpreter and a researcher, you also own a thriving translation and interpreting agency. What have you learned about adding value to clients while running the agency?

I own and run fifteen translation agencies. From the role of the business owner, and also from my roles as a researcher and an interpreter, I've learned that the ability to listen is the most important. By listening, you not only make the client feel important and valued, but you also identify the real needs of the client in order to provide tailor-made services. Interpreting is not a 'one size fits all' profession. The services of the interpreter should be tailor-made to meet the clients' needs and expectations.

Some interpreters are quite wary of agencies for one reason or another. In what ways do you feel that agencies and interpreters could work together to add value?

I feel that both freelancers and agency owners should try to look at the issues at hand from both sides. Agencies should value their freelancers, and thus train, listen, and reward them accordingly. Freelancers should appreciate that agency owners took a risk by investing into a business, and face multifaceted challenges and expenses. Therefore, freelancers should not prejudge agencies as the 'bad employers' who just make money out of their work.

Both interpreters and agency owners should learn to work together toward the same target, which is high-quality service provision. Services can be improved only if all sides contribute their individual (and collective) knowledge, ideas, and perspectives. Adequate and relevant information should be passed both ways (by interpreters to agencies and vice versa) in order for the profession to move forward and progress.

The central argument of this chapter is that interpreters need to leave behind the traditional idea of neutrality and focus on adding value. Where do you stand on that issue?

Neutrality is a problematic concept on its own. Can someone ever be truly neutral? Personally, I do not believe in neutrality. As human beings, we have our own references and prejudices. Even if we try to be neutral, all the information that we receive and transmit is filtered through these references and prejudices. If we interpreters want to add value to our services, especially in liaison settings, we should try to decode more than words, and transmit emotions, feelings, cultural elements and every other aspect or route of communication that clients would be able to understand if they belonged to the same culture and the same language as the other speaker. By not providing the interpretation of the paralinguistic and extra-linguistic elements, interpreters are actually concealing communicative cues and are thus acting unethically. Obviously, that practice is not advisable for all settings, but in business-negotiation settings, my area of expertise, it is paramount.

A concern has been expressed that leaving behind neutrality makes it more likely that interpreters will favour one side or another. Do you agree that this may be an issue and why?

I believe that interpreters do favour one party, even if it is unconsciously. What interpreters should not do is show this 'preference' in their interpretation by misleading, misinterpreting, or altering something that is said. We are there to facilitate communication for both or all parties involved. For some interpreting settings, such as court interpreting, favouring one party or another is an unprofessional thing to do. In other settings, like business settings, it is expected that the interpreter will favour and team up with the fee-paying party, and that is why in big negotiation deals there are as many interpreters as negotiation parties.

What piece of advice would you give to interpreters who really want to add value and demonstrate that they add value to their clients?

Do not just be a conduit. Use common sense, listen carefully, ask before acting out of the 'traditional role', and try to offer the services needed by clients (within reason). Remember that you are present in a communicative event in order to facilitate communication, and communication involves more than just words.

Key chapter concepts

- The 'something' that clients are looking for is that ability to make the event or report or consultation better or more effective than it would have been without you.
- If we are not delivering what clients really want then we need to change our approach.
- What if, instead of making accuracy and impartiality non-negotiable, we make it our goal to work with our clients to deliver an event that fulfils its purpose?
- Partnership in the success of others will always be the best way to persuade them to hire you again.
- By listening, you not only make the client feel important and valued, but you also identify the real needs of the client in order to provide tailor-made services.

Putting it into practice

This section aims to help you put the ideas from this chapter into practice in your own work. As with every chapter, ideas begin with questions to ask, before moving into actions to take. The first step, of course, is to look at our role as individuals. Only after that can we move to work we can do in groups.

Questions to ask

How comfortable are you with the idea of adding value to clients? Take a few minutes to think about the reasons for your answer.

Thinking about your last interpreting assignment, how important do you think you were to your clients' success or to the success of the event as a whole? Do you think your clients would say the same thing?

When preparing for an assignment, how much time do you spend thinking about what your clients will want from the event?

In the settings you usually work in, what do you think added-value interpreting would look like?

Actions to take

On your own

For your next assignment, take time to think of how your clients would know that the event had been a success. Try to brainstorm ways that you could sensibly help the event to succeed.

Take an inventory of the kinds of organisations and settings within which you work and the kinds of people you work with. Try to find out what publications are read by people in the organisations and settings and read some of them yourself. What are their concerns? What do they see as important?

Once you know more about the way your clients think, use that knowledge in your preparation for your next assignment. Put yourself in their shoes and imagine how you would want the interpreter to act, work, and add value.

In a group

Find interpreters who work for similar clients to you and go to a tradeshow or seminar in that area together. Spend time talking to those there about their work, experience with interpreters, and what they want out of the events at which you normally work. Share your findings with each other.

Work with other interpreters in an informal group or as part of a wider association to gather stories of how interpreters have added value to their clients. Prepare anonymised versions of the stories and look for ways to publish them in places your clients will see.

Find some other interpreters working in the same setting whom you can trust and meet with regularly online or in person to discuss the best and most appropriate ways to add value to the clients you work with.

Notes

1 Franz Pöchhacker, 'Conference Interpreting: Surveying the Profession', *Translation and Interpreting Studies*, 4, no. 2 (2009): 181. doi:10.1075/tis.4.2.02poc.
2 Cornelia Zwischenberger, 'Simultaneous Conference Interpreting and a Supernorm That Governs It All', *Meta: Journal Des traducteurs/ Meta: Translators' Journal*, 60, no. 1 (2015): 90–111.
3 See E. Diriker, *De-/Re-Contextualizing Conference Interpreting: Interpreters in the Ivory Tower?*, vol. 53 (Amsterdam: John Benjamins Publishing Company, 2004), 25–50.
4 Robyn K. Dean, 'Condemned to Repetition? An Analysis of Problem-Setting and Problem-Solving in Sign Language Interpreting Ethics', *Translation & Interpreting*, 6, no. 1 (2014): 60–75.
5 Jonathan Downie, 'What Every Client Wants?(Re) Mapping the Trajectory of Client Expectations Research', *Meta: Journal Des traducteurs/ Meta: Translators' Journal*, 60, no. 1 (2015): 18–35.

6 Şeyda Eraslan, '"Cultural Mediator" or "Scrupulous Translator"? Revisiting Role, Context and Culture in Consecutive Conference Interpreting', ed. Pieter Boulogne, in *Translation and Its Others. Selected Papers of the CETRA Research Seminar in Translation Studies 2007*, 2008; 'International Knowledge Transfer in Turkey: The Consecutive Interpreter's Role in Context' (Unpublished Doctoral Thesis, Rovira i Virgili University, 2011).
7 María Gracia Torres Díaz and Alessandro Ghignoli, 'Interpreting Performed by Professionals of Other Fields: The Case of Sports Commentators' (The Second Conference on Non-Professional Interpreting and Translation (NPIT2), Germersheim, Germany, 2014). Retrieved from http://dspace.uma.es/xmlui/handle/10630/8130.
8 Graham H. Turner, 'Towards Real Interpreting', in *Sign Language Interpreting and Interpreter Education: Directions for Research and Practice*, ed. M. Marschark, R. Peterson, and E. Winston (New York: Oxford University Press, 2005), 253–65.

Chapter 2

Masters of our future

Initial training for a new breed of interpreters

Chapter summary

This chapter covers:

*   Why experienced professionals need to care about initial training,
*   The truth about interpreting that every course must cover,
*   Why a degree, on its own, will never be enough.

Why should established interpreters care about training? We've all had our share of training, and perhaps thought about training others. A few of us might like to supplement our income by taking on the odd class, but that's likely the limit of our interest.

The very fact that this chapter exists means that you should expect me to make a case that initial training, whether it takes place in universities, colleges, or via independent providers, is far more important for established professionals than we might think. In fact, unless professional interpreters become more structured and intentional in their relationships with training providers, they will reduce their ability to provide value to their clients.

To understand how this works, one can learn from a profession with a longer history. In the training of nurses, attention is increasingly moving from the content of initial training courses to the need to create structures that make sure that graduates are set up to continually develop as professionals during and after their training. Nursing trainer Ann Cummins gathered together the available evidence and concluded that the future supply of excellent nurses depends on a successful handover of new graduates from nursing schools to supportive supervision arrangements in the workplace[1]. In other words, for the good of patients and the profession, nurses need to be trained and supported to keep learning after they have graduated.

Much the same lesson can be learned in interpreter training. To be absolutely fair, most interpreting training programs, whether they are at degree level or done via short courses, do their best to try to prepare students for the world they will soon enter. Research since the 1960s has sought to discover how students can be trained to work with excellence. We are used to the idea that interpreter education has to cover all the bases: note-taking, ethics, equipment, assignment preparation, information management, text analysis, and the list goes on.

Yet, if initial training is about producing people who can walk into the workplace and function as professionals, there are two key requirements. If graduates are to survive as interpreters, they need to be competent in business and integrated into the values and mores of the professional interpreting community.

In terms of business skills, the first priority will always be ensuring the right number and mix of clients. Given the continued growth in international trade made possible by the internet, interpreters need to know how to market themselves to clients who might not even know the difference between translation and interpreting. Since in-house interpreting is now the sole province of a few international organisations, interpreters will need to know how to balance income and expenses, submit tax forms, and mind the bottom line.

In preparing interpreters for work, we need to prepare them for the reality that a large proportion of their time will be taken up doing the things that businesspeople do. Administrative, marketing, and accounting duties are just as vital for the aspiring professional as the ability to build a term list from a few odd websites and an incomplete Wikipedia page.

There is, of course, much more to interpreting than simply getting clients and getting paid, but those two subjects have only fairly recently started appearing regularly in interpreting degree programs, and for good reason. Anyone who has tried to compile even a basic list of skills needed by interpreters will realise that it is a daunting job to teach even half of them in a two-year Master's course. Does anyone exit their degree thinking that their note-taking skills are world leading? Do any recent graduates feel that they have learned all there is to know about term research or turn taking or *décalage* management?

The traditional view, at least in Europe, was to assume that the needs of the big international organisations would deal with any remaining issues anyway. In that view, it was the job of universities to prepare students to work for the biggest, most prestigious clients (governments and international organisations) and then to advise students to jump through whatever hoops were necessary to pick up such work. In this paradigm, there is no need for marketing or community building, as interpreters essentially become staff members. They have a limited number of clients (perhaps only one) and become so well known there that they will have no worries for the future.

That was all well and good until fairly recently. There was great merit in making sure that students were prepared for those markets, as those markets seemed poised for growth, or at least sufficient maintenance to accommodate a few newcomers. At some point in the recent past, however, those assumptions were demolished. The number of courses in interpreting ballooned. The rates for government contracts imploded, and those in staff positions decided that they could still work for a few more years . . . or ten.

No matter how many adverts the big organisations place for staff jobs, supply will always outstrip demand. No matter how hard interpreter associations campaign, there is little prospect of the salaries of community interpreters meeting those of doctors, at least not in the near future.

So what now?

The only answer seems to be to do some hard-headed calculations and adjust our expectations. For most interpreters reading this, the future is likely to involve more work with agencies and a focus on marketing oneself to gain direct clients rather than taxpayer-subsidised trips to Brussels or Washington, DC. It is even probable that many of our newest and best clients will know less about interpreting than we did before we started our degrees. Some level of compromise and negotiation will be needed, and that is before interpreters even leave the house.

With that in mind, interpreters need to adjust their expectations for initial education, as much as, if not more than, those courses will need to adjust their syllabi. Possessing a diploma or Master's degree in interpreting will soon be the equivalent of holding a passport: it will allow you to be waved across the border, but the cost of the trip to and from that border is still yours to pay.

Concretely, there is a growing realisation that the best universities can do is to give interpreters in training the skills and mindsets that will be needed to start the journey to professionalism. Critical thinking, group work, problem solving, and, yes, technical skills, like note-taking and conversation management, are all necessary starting points. Finding one's own way toward continued professional development (see Chapter 3) and building excellence in marketing, finance, and sales, as well as locating an interpreting community to join and contribute to, propel us farther along the journey.

That is not to say the universities shouldn't offer courses on the business end of interpreting. In writing this chapter, and especially in doing the interview with Kirsty Heimerl-Moggan, I found out, to my happy surprise, that the landscape is changing. Anthony Pym pointed out that it is tricky to talk about typical degrees nowadays, as the syllabi differ so widely, with marketing and business skills very much on the agenda[2].

Universities are also increasingly becoming aware of the need for pro-active partnership with the rest of the interpreting industry. It is now normal for university programs to include some level of input from practising professionals, whether those professionals are doing the teaching or appearing at end-of-course events. It would be surprising if the near future does not include the formalisation of such links in the form of mutual certification: the national and international interpreting associations putting their stamp of approval on excellent courses and universities granting some level of credit for previous CPD.

Indeed, national associations are beginning to realise that there are some skills that are better 'caught' than taught. Mentoring is growing in popularity. So long as this growth proves sustainable, we could see a new model of interpreter training where universities offer students their initial training, and established professionals take graduates under their wing and guide them the rest of the way.

For the good of the profession, such two-way cooperation must be encouraged and supported. If we are going to see interpreters adding value to their clients, there has to be a continuing dialogue between the trainers, the trainees, and the already trained as to what the most relevant skills are and how those with experience can contribute to developing the profession.

And this is where the readers of this book come in. The students who are in training courses right now are your future colleagues. Perhaps you are one of them. What kind of colleagues do we want? What kind of interpreter communities can we build to make sure that we support, counsel, and guide those who are new to the profession so they don't fall into the low-rates/low-status trap, but instead pro-actively help to push the profession forward? What can we add to the training that is already on offer?

If we really want a strong, powerful profession, our vision needs to be even broader than the courses themselves. Much like medical and nursing training involves supervised, hands-on placements that become longer and eventually morph into supervised practice after graduation, student interpreters and the entire profession would benefit from a system of managed placements, especially in cases where interpreter training takes place at the undergraduate level.

For those working on Master's and diploma courses, placements during the course will always be challenging, but mentoring can offer a useful compromise. In conference interpreting, we all work with boothmates, anyway; perhaps you can serve as a mentor to your boothmate. There is always the possibility of taking just one job per year and choosing to work with a newer interpreter so he or she gets the vital experience that's needed. In other forms of interpreting, more creativity will be needed. We could start by creating structures that allow interpreters to discuss work issues and decision making, normalising the idea that senior interpreters might take newer entrants to the field under their wing, and even copying the medical professions by finding ways to have new interpreters shadow more experienced colleagues. None of these things will be achieved overnight, but they will go a long way toward the improvement in professional status that we all seem to desire.

If this chapter seems short, it is not because this is an easy topic or one that is easily solved. The challenge for everyone reading this is to work out how they can contribute. From the largest association to the newest student, everyone has a part to play in the continual development of training and education that offers students useful and relevant instruction and experience that gives them the skills to start their journey toward adding value to clients and their profession. Individual interpreters, informal communities, and large associations all have their parts to play alongside universities if this goal is to be achieved and all stand to benefit.

When it comes to courses that prepare interpreters for the future, you can't go wrong if you have an experienced interpreter for a teacher or mentor, especially one who is passionate about helping future colleagues to develop their skills. Kirsty Heimerl-Moggan fits this bill exactly, and has a reputation for being a skilled teacher and nurturing mentor. It was a pleasure to interview her for this chapter.

Interview with Kirsty Heimerl-Moggan

You manage to combine interpreting, research, and teaching in two countries. How did you get to that stage and how do you manage it?

I have been an interpreter for over twenty years but I can most definitely say that I did not get to the stage of combining all these tasks early on in my career. I always say to my students, "Give yourself at least two years before you can expect jobs to come in on a more regular basis and not just on the odd occasion". After graduation it took two years for the first few of my interpreting assignments to come in, and then over the next year or so I gradually eased myself into self-employment as an interpreter.

The teaching came about when there was a vacancy at my old university, and I was therefore gradually eased into teaching interpreting. Over the next couple of years I left my old university to go and teach conference interpreting briefly at Leeds University and before being appointed to my present post at UCLan (University of Central Lancashire). And more recently, I have also taught at Munich University of Applied Languages, in Germany.

What really helps me juggle my many commitments is that I absolutely adore my job as an interpreter. I love the buzz I get from working in the booth, and even now I still get excited when a new job comes through, as all I ever wanted to be was an interpreter. I also find working in all the diverse areas of interpreting, such as conference interpreting, business interpreting, and public-service interpreting, gives the job real variety.

Could you explain a little about the content of the courses you teach at UCLan? What areas of interpreting practice and business skills do you emphasise?

I ended up at the University of Central Lancashire because I was actually recommended by a colleague of mine who already worked there. I asked the dean of school for all the means to start 'the perfect course' from scratch, like state-of-the-art booths, colleagues for each language who were practising interpreters, and free reign as far as designing the course went. Much to my surprise, I was given half a year to create the course and all my 'demands' were met and I was actually given the go-ahead to put the course together just the way I chose.

I had become very disillusioned with the lack of practical aspects incorporated in the interpreter training at MA level at my first university. There seemed to be no recognition of how vital 'real life' input is to a good interpreting course. At Leeds University, I experienced the value of using practising professionals. So I decided to make the simultaneous and consecutive interpreting modules at UCLan as hands-on and realistic as possible by using actual materials from real-life interpreting assignments with relevant up-to-date topics. What I was missing when I started working were the very business skills that you mention. So I dedicated a module that runs across thirty weeks solely aimed at developing business skills in students.

In the business module we actually teach them how to create invoices and to set up and maintain their accounts. We invite professional entities to come and speak to them and advise them on the do's and don'ts of the job. We have workshops on using social media, creating your LinkedIn profile, and the like. We even give them advice on how to deal with their taxes, how to create a good CV, and how to design their own website.

Could you give some examples of how your professional experience has affected your teaching?

We have weekly topics on the course and, much as they are quite loosely outlined, we do give certain ideas of what the exact topics may be so that students can prepare. My practical professional experience often affects my teaching in that I have brand-new, up-to-date materials that I can use on the students (obviously ensuring that the client has given permission beforehand and there is nothing confidential being divulged).

My professional experience also impacts on my lessons in other ways: I take students with me to interpreting assignments, either to work with me or to observe a colleague and me interpreting.

Finally, my students benefit very strongly from anything that occurs during my assignments because I share it with them if something has gone well or wrong during an assignment. This ensures that they don't make the same mistakes and gives them a chance to replicate anything that worked very well.

And how does your research affect your teaching?

I am currently undertaking research in consecutive interpreting, more specifically note-taking in public-service interpreting. The idea was that traditional research in conference interpreter note-taking would be applied to public-service interpreting where note-taking is far less established. What has actually happened is that my research into public-service interpreter note-taking is now feeding into my conference-interpreting teaching as it turns out that it is extremely useful for the non–Western European languages in conference interpreting. More on that when my PhD is complete and published.

Have you seen any changes in how interpreting is taught since you started teaching?

The changes to teaching since I underwent training and later began teaching interpreting have been huge. To some extent I find it quite embarrassing when I think back to what used to be taught (and I am not excluding myself here!). The focus was on teaching techniques, like simultaneous and consecutive, combined with huge amounts of theory. In part this will have been due to the fact that most teachers of interpreting were not interpreters or were, at best, retired interpreters, with some exceptions to the rule of course.

Job specs for interpreting lecturers now include relevant interpreting experience, teaching experience/training (e.g. PGCE), and research. This makes the staff who are teaching budding interpreters into true all-rounders, and therefore, I dare say, much better teachers.

Even a look at the development of my own teaching since I started nearly two decades ago makes me cringe somewhat. Comparing what I taught in the early stages of my teaching career to what I teach now makes it clear that the current calibre of my teaching is very different from what it was then. It is easy to see how the changes and improvements I have made over the years (mostly based on my real-life interpreting experience) have a positive impact on the learning experience of my students.

Lastly, what advice would you give to practising interpreters who want to help students prepare for life after their degrees?

There are a number of things I would advise practising interpreters who want to help students prepare for life after their degrees. One of the mistakes I made in the early days was to assume that everyone would learn in the same way I did. Now I would say don't assume just because you have the experience in interpreting you will necessarily initially be a very good teacher.

Even if you are a very good interpreter, you should listen to your students – I have learnt so much from my students over the years. Once you realise that you are simply bringing your own colleagues into the job, you're onto a winner be-cause you can adapt and use different approaches and methods to teach the students based on real-life interpreting experience.

Some further advice would be to not forget that you were at the beginner's stage yourself once. Teaching requires selflessness and giving a lot of yourself. It is im-portant not to see yourself as basically breeding your competition. If you have enough confidence in your own abilities, you need not worry about your former students 'stealing' your jobs. Quite the contrary: I now have some brilliant and successful booth partners that I love working with and 99 per cent of them are my former students!

Key chapter concepts

- Unless we become more structured and intentional in our relationships with training providers, we will reduce our ability to provide value to our clients.
- Interpreters are businesspeople.
- No matter how many adverts the big organisations place for staff jobs, supply will always outstrip demand.
- If we are going to see interpreters adding value to their clients, there has to be a continuing dialogue between the trainers, the trainees, and the trained as to

what the most relevant skills are and how those with experience under their belts can contribute.

- Don't forget that you were at the beginner's stage yourself once.

Putting it into practice

Questions to ask

What was your experience of university training? Did it prepare you adequately for your work?

If you could go back and redesign your degree course, what would you include?

How much of an interest do you take in the way that interpreters are trained?

Actions to take

On your own

Find the contact details for your local interpreter training department. Offer to do a talk on what it is like to be a practising professional to students. If you want to go the extra mile, ask if you can practise alongside the students for one or two classes.

Blog about your university experience and invite other people to discuss theirs.

Offer your services as a mentor to one or two new graduates.

In a group

There are two levels to this, since informal groups of interpreters are in a very different position than professional associations.

Informal groups are in a great position to arrange mentoring, since they can move quickly and share experience effectively. You might want to create an informal forum for networking and development or even just invite newer interpreters out for a coffee. Whatever it is, concentrate on starting small and really getting to know new interpreters before helping them to develop in a way that suits them.

Professional associations, on the other hand, are in a great position to create formal ties with universities, exercising real influence over what courses cover and how this meshes with their own development tracks. Interpreting really does need both national and regional associations to not just relay information to universities but listen to them too, utilizing structures that take the needs of both group types into account.

For those who run professional associations, building formal mentoring programs, approving excellent degrees, and adjusting membership criteria according to the ways interpreters actually develop are all ways of making a big difference to our industry. Each of these steps comes with its own challenges and pitfalls, but all of them have the potential to revolutionise interpreting for the better.

Notes

1 Ann Cummins, 'Clinical Supervision: The Way Forward? A Review of the Literature', *Nurse Education in Practice*, *9*, no. 3 (2009): 215–20.
2 Anthony Pym, 'Translator Training', in *Oxford Companion to Translation Studies*, 2009. Retrieved from www.researchgate.net/profile/Anthony_Pym2/publication/242711915_Translator_training/links/53fd94050cf2dca8000353cf.pdf.

Chapter 3

Can professionals develop?

Growing as professionals after we graduate

Chapter summary

This chapter covers:

- Why continued professional development (CPD) is a necessity, not an option,
- What CPD is and how to do it intelligently,
- How to put together a growth plan.

It was all supposed to be so perfect. I had the degree, I had the time, and I had an unlimited broadband connection. I thought I had everything I needed to be the world's most successful interpreter and translator – cue the victorious rock anthem.

In reality, my situation proved to be more like hearing a typical 7-year-old practice the violin than seeing U2 play a victorious rock anthem. For about six months, I quoted for every translation or interpreting job I could possibly do, and even attempted some pretty borderline cases. I bought business cards. I even tried linking up with a secretariat in Paris.

The response was, to put it Britishly, rather disappointing. My tax records show that I started officially in January, but it would be late March before anyone displayed any interest in working with me. Even then, I landed my first job more on the strength of having recently signed a lease and knowing what they looked like than due to any of the skills I had practiced so hard during university.

As much as I would have been loath to admit it, I had no clue what I was doing. I didn't understand the different ways of marketing my skills. I didn't know what kinds of clients I wanted, and I had no clue about leveraging my online presence to make money.

It would take me a couple of years of frustration to realise that somehow I needed to find ways to learn from other professionals. There is something about having a Master's degree that makes it more difficult to admit that you need help, but the truth is that none of us would get very far without assistance from our colleagues.

The problem is only made worse by some of the attitudes that have developed in the history of interpreting. As I mentioned in Chapter 2, most of us came through educational systems that were geared toward producing staff interpreters for large international organisations. If we didn't become staffers, we were expected to launch into the existing systems for managing interpreting in large conference cities and work our way up the same ladder that interpreters have been building for the past fifty years.

Undoubtedly, there is some value in that system. For interpreters who can make it to the large international organisations, income is likely to be steady, clients are likely to be reliable, and marketing is likely to be taken care of by others. But what if your market is much less organised? What if you live in a city dominated by combative agencies, and most potential clients look to save money at every turn? What if we find that the current protective systems are not quite sustainable, and we can't grab our little slice of pre-existing markets and settle down to cosy normality?

The truth is that we all need to be continually working on all our skills, from sharpening our sim technique to mastering marketing. Without adequate *business* skills, interpreters have little to no chance of getting paid appropriately for their services. Without sufficient *interpreting* skills, we won't get paid period, or at least not twice by the same client.

Yet it doesn't seem that practising those skills, or continued professional development, is seen as a value of our profession. Interpreters talk a lot about neutrality and impartiality, but how many stress the importance of expecting themselves and their colleagues to continually sharpen their skills? How many would be happy to see a commitment to a certain number of hours becoming a condition of membership of our professional associations?

In reading the work of Elisabet Tiselius[1], one might suspect that we as a profession have forgotten that key mindset. Go to any other profession and those who are deemed experts in it have reached that level by deliberate practice: working on specific areas of their performance with specific targets and with the help of a coach or mentor. Doctors spend time training under other doctors, musicians work with teachers and conductors, sports people pay huge sums for professional coaching. Interpreters, however, watch a few YouTube videos, produce a term list, and call it done.

Granted, what qualifies as continued professional development for interpreters can get murky. Tiselius reminds us that interpreters can participate in a wide range of activities, from watching TV in one's B language to taking speech-therapy sessions, and call those activities CPD or 'practice'[2]. We can and do read newspapers, browse encyclopaedias, and read journals to increase our knowledge. Unlike doctors or lawyers, interpreters are expected to have enviable general knowledge, and so they really can say that watching the news in Portuguese is helping them work more effectively.

Even so, something is missing. Tiselius points out that experts in other fields don't simply practice; they set goals and work with coaches. A fellow professional helps them to set targets, monitor progress, and evaluate their work. This type of accountability is something that doesn't come from webinars or conferences. It takes building relationships and risking vulnerability.

Now it would seem logical that interpreters, who tend to be extroverts and seem to like to talk, would relish this kind of accountability, correct? In truth, the more common outcome would be to get worried looks or confused shrugs in response to a request for help. Colleagues might wonder, 'Doesn't he already have the right skills? Should she really be working if there are skills she still has to hone?'

Interpreters seem to have built up a culture where it is normal to give off an aura of polished perfection. Who is this attitude really serving? We can seem as polished as we like, but the reality of your skill set will always reveal itself. Pity the poor interpreter who comes across as the epitome of perfection and yet struggles with the guest speaker's jokes or the president's reference to a local national monument. Even worse, imagine failing to relay the passion of the speaker due to shortcomings in public-speaking technique and hiding behind neutrality and objectivity. 'Well I got the meaning across' is not an excuse that clients, or colleagues will accept.

If interpreting is to go from a cost item to a value-added service, we need to address our fear of growth (or the lack thereof) in a deliberate manner. If interpreting is to be seen as a value-added service, interpreters need to make skill development and growth a normal, even expected, part of professional life.

Let me be very specific about what I mean by 'growth'. I do not mean that interpreters should simply go to CPD courses, take massive open online courses (MOOCs), and/or add another language. Those actions can certainly be beneficial, but they often have limited impact unless they are part of a bigger plan. Unless you have a clear sense of direction, the effect of any single activity will be limited.

We might all be vaguely aware that setting learning goals is important, but few of us seem to fully understand why that is the case. Research verifies that the setting of learning goals positively impacts the goal setter's desired outcome. For example, in 1998, a team from Southern Methodist University in the US showed that salespeople who set goals for their *learning* tended to perform better monetarily than those who simply set goals for the amount of sales they wanted[3].

Interpreters might acknowledge the need for CPD and even attend a few courses, but how many could actually tell others who their coaches and mentors were? How many have, in the last month, sought specific help to grow in a measurable way in an area of their professional interpreting practice? How many actually have a plan for what they want to learn and why? In the previous chapter, I argued for supervision of new graduates and for that supervision to play a central part of their training. Here, I want to make the point that this type of close supervision and growth accountability is something all interpreters need.

So when I talk about growth, I mean deliberate and targeted growth in one or more specific areas that are relevant to your practice, preferably with some kind of accountability in place. Personally, at this time, I have targeted three areas to develop. Firstly, I know my business skills need to be refined, especially as regards marketing and new client acquisition. Generally, this translates to a big proportion of this year's CPD time going into networking, updated marketing techniques, and a revamp of my online presence. Specifically, I want to attend at least one networking event a month; apply the lessons from Judy and Dagmar Jenner's book, *The Entrepreneurial Linguist*, by revamping my website with its own URL, new images, and content; and create new business cards.

My second big area for growth is my French presentation skills. For this, I will be employing several somewhat more passive methods, such as listening to and watching more French speakers while making notes on their techniques, spending more time with resources that will develop my French, and deliberately immersing myself in French prose. So, it's out with the BBC for a while and in with *Le Figaro*, *Le Monde*, and *L'Express*.

My third area to develop is my language repertoire. My goal is to add, or at least begin to add, a new language. In my case, due to a project on the horizon that involves lots of travel to Germany, my new language will be German. I already have a bit of a start after having taken two years of university-level courses, but since then I have stagnated a bit, and I know it is time to invest fifteen to twenty minutes most days to work on my knowledge of German.

Notice that I have been very specific about what areas I want to develop and have set goals for skill development in each. Some of these goals are simply about the amount of time spent; others are about the end results. It is also likely that I will find that I have some weeks when I feel I've made gains in all three areas and other weeks when I feel that I've let those goals slip a bit. That's okay. I am more interested in progress than perfection, especially since the latter is impossible anyway! My aim is that every working day will involve some amount of time on at least one of these areas, no matter how busy I am.

These goals aren't listed here to make me look good. Quite the contrary, I am sure some readers will have read them a bit disapprovingly, thinking perhaps, 'Doesn't he already have excellent marketing skills? Should he really be interpreting if his French presentation skills need work?'

The point in listing my goals is simply to illustrate what growth looks like. Growth is difficult and often slow. It involves admitting areas in which you need help and seeking to find that help. It means putting some time aside for yourself and your goals, even on your busiest days. Growth means accountability and, often, spending money too.

But what is the alternative? Let's go back to Elisabet Tiselius and her work. Her PhD[4] includes some of the most shocking results I have ever seen. In one of the studies she carried out, she asked three staff interpreters working in international organisations to reinterpret a speech they had worked on fifteen years earlier. Comparing the recordings of the two versions, she found that none of the interpreters she studied had shown any sign of improvement over that time – in fact, one even seemed to have gotten worse!

The alternative to growth is stagnation – the kind of stagnation that struggles to survive market shifts and budget cuts; the kind of stagnation that can't work with new technology, even when it is much better; the kind of stagnation that refuses to add value because 'that's not my job'. If the future development, and even survival, of interpreting has an enemy, it is stagnation. You can name any change you like in our working practices and clients – remote interpreting, pay changes, aging demographics, globalisation, onshoring/offshoring, virtualisation – and the only way to face them and still thrive is to work hard to avoid stagnation.

The overarching theme of this book is adding value, and the only way we can achieve that is through growth. If you want to know what interpreters will be like in five or ten years, just look at the interpreters we have now and imagine them deliberately growing.

At the end of this chapter, I challenge you to put together your own growth plan and find someone to keep you accountable. I also challenge those who have power in professional associations to 'hit the pause button' on some activities in order to privilege activities that will promote growth amongst their members. Before that, however, I want to give you an insight into the person whose work inspired this chapter. Here, then, is my interview with Dr Elisabet Tiselius.

Interview with Elisabet Tiselius

Elisabet, your work has challenged some of our pre-existing views of what it means to grow and develop as an interpreter. Could you tell us what inspired your PhD?

I heard a talk by Edvard Moser, the 2014 Nobel Prize laureate for medicine. He said that he probably became a researcher because he was always questioning the 'truth'. In my case, it was the awe and admiration I felt for several of my senior colleagues. They were such wizards, and I desperately wanted to learn what they had learnt and understand how they did it. I certainly didn't want to settle for the then quite common explanation that some people 'just had it'. So, I would say that in my case it was curiosity, but also a certain challenge of the 'truth'. But, I also have to admit that it was still difficult to accept, towards the end of my project, that what I had until then accepted as truth maybe wasn't.

One of the most surprising results was that there seemed to be no difference in the quality of work produced by interpreters even after they had gained fifteen years additional experience. Why do you think this is?

Yes, this was the new truth that I had to learn to accept and understand how it could happen. Unfortunately, nothing is ever as straightforward in research as you would have liked it to be, but in short there could be two reasons for this.

1   Maybe my instruments were too blunt: most research that investigates the development of expertise (including my own previous studies) is done on different groups, i.e. the beginners and the experienced participants are different people. My research is the first, and to my knowledge the only one in in-

terpreting, that actually investigates the *same* individuals' development over time. So if this explanation is true, then maybe none of the previous research is valid, because then we do not know whether the difference is due to inter-individual variation and not experience or expertise.

2   Maybe the participants were 'only' very skilled routine experts. This means that they are very good at what they are doing in a particular context, but that when the context changes then the expert knowledge fades away (the speech that compared them to their younger selves was outside their current context). Arguments against this are that this group did not do very well compared to the control group of very experienced interpreters when they interpreted a speech within their expert context. I would like to stress, though, that they did not do *badly*, just not as well as I would have expected, and certainly not outperforming themselves as students.

What is interesting here is why they did not do as well as expected. They had all the external signs of excellence – accreditation to institutions, membership in professional organizations, renowned for being good interpreters, and still. . . . A bad day? Not engaging in the exercise? Or simply not as good as I thought? An interesting common denominator was that they all were very clear about not practicing outside their booth work. All of them talked about different things they did, which I ended up labelling them 'skill enhancing techniques', to become better interpreters, but none of them would label it practice and none of them spent time in the booth, without working, only practicing the main skill (i.e. not adding a new language, but just working on improving your existing skill). The question that then arises is: if we don't label it practice, does it have the same effect on the end product?

People often quote the idea that if you spend 10,000 hours practising something, you will become an expert. What is your take on that?

Can I swear? I think it's total rubbish! On top of that, I believe it is a very patronizing way of telling people and especially young people and children 'you didn't work long enough or hard enough, so you didn't make it'. It puts all the blame on the person or child who did not reach a certain goal. Finally it is undermining the expert skill. There's so much more to expertise than just spending 10,000 hours on a task. The expertise paradigm[5] does not put the amount of training in a very prominent place for achieving expert knowledge. Clearly, you do not become very skilled at anything unless you spend a large amount of time exercising whatever you would like to excel in. However, you can spend an impressive amount of hours doing things without becoming an expert. I usually take myself as example; I have easily spent 10,000 hours cooking food for the past thirty years or so. I believe my family should eat good and healthy food, so I actually put both time and effort into cooking. There is only one problem – I don't like cooking, and despite all those years, and the effort, I'm at best an ordinary cook, and often a really bad one. No one I know would compare my cooking to Bocuse. Ramsay would never hire me. Yet, I have spent 10,000 hours on a task. Now, I dare you to tell me that just because I didn't work hard enough . . .

Often students leave their initial training thinking that they have learned all they need to learn. How can we counteract that thinking?

We can counteract that in the way we train the students. Athletes and musicians learn that unless they practice they will not be able to pursue their career; they learn it both from their teachers and coaches, and the hard way. Researchers are taught that unless they continue their research they will quickly be sidestepped. But, when I try to analyse what we do as interpreting teachers, I have the impression that students are told to practice but not taught to practice. Learning to practice must be part of the curriculum. Furthermore, students are not taught lifelong learning. Lifelong learning is a buzzword now, and for most interpreters it has always been a reality when it comes to keeping up with current affairs, learning new topics, or new languages. But I have the impression that this is not true when it comes to the components that build up our main skill (voice, intonation, transfer, pace, and so forth).

Some people in the field of interpreting have started to argue that continued professional development is so important that it should be seen as a necessary part of being a practising interpreter. Would you be happy for it to be seen this way?

Mostly yes. Many professional associations (e.g. American Translators Association; ATA) have requirements to fulfil a certain amount of CPD points every year, and many of them also organize CPD. I like that, but if you are not part of a professional association, which will then control the CPD, our clients will most likely not look at our CPD portfolio. Universities and interpreting programs could play a more important role here though, and organize shorter courses for active interpreters. And finally, I think that the benefits of CPD are also something we need to teach.

If you were advising new interpreters to choose specific areas to target for their growth, which ones would you choose and why?

I will not go into marketing, negotiation, and other business-related areas, which are also vital for new interpreters. I stick to interpreting skills, such as the following:

1   Voice training – Actors take voice classes or work with voice coaches. I don't understand why teachers and interpreters and other 'voice professions' don't. Interpreting programs give voice training, but again, it seems to be perceived as a one-off phenomenon, and once you've finished your program you think you know it.

2 Presentation skills – Interpreting is about presentation, and your presentation skills can always be improved. And, the better you are at presentations, the better you can follow the speaker, too. You can learn to master different types of presentations when it comes to both topic and style (Pecha Kucha, just to mention one).

3 Working with a mentor or coach – You may not agree with me, but I don't think interpreters are very good at mentorship or coaching. And most feedback is based on you missed this word or that argument. But good mentors or good coaches can do so much more. Obviously, you don't have to work with a coach every day or week, but on a regular basis would probably be beneficial. Again think actors or musicians.

Which growth areas do you think more experienced interpreters might need to target and why?

As a matter of fact, I think that the points above go for interpreters of all levels of experience. I think it should be part of the lifelong learning.

I argue in this chapter that often it can be difficult for interpreters to admit their weaknesses and get help. How would you suggest we overcome this tendency?

The million-euro question. Unfortunately, the world of interpreting is not necessarily a warm, open, generous world. We are all competitors for the same assignments. Furthermore, unless you are convinced that you are right (and sometimes also outstanding), you cannot convince your listener. These two factors together make it difficult for interpreters to admit weaknesses and work on them. Once again, I believe in the new generations and the training we give them. I believe in the 'community of practice' approach, something I try to establish at my university, and which Danielle D'Hayer is working with too, and doing research on for interpreters, and which has been launched as a digital initiative by eCPD[6], too. But training programs can also help here; so far I have not heard of brush-up courses (only focusing on technique) for active interpreters.

One of the common issues that people raise with work on the development and growth of interpreters is that such studies often involve small numbers. How representative do you think studies such as yours might be of wider trends in the profession?

I would like to answer with an example. The research on the patient H.M., who had undergone lobectomy and as a consequence lost his long-term memory, contributed enormously to the research on brain function and memory, cognitive neuropsychology, and specific psychological processes. But H.M. was the only participant in those studies and for research studies that is a very small number. My argument is that it is not necessarily the number of participants in the study that impacts representativity, but rather how you use your material, what type of conclusions you draw, and what happens after the study. Empirical material does not mean big data, empirical means that you are using a scientifically collected and analysed material, and not just reporting your own experience or opinion. In my case, my study is only an indication, and it has to be followed up with more participants, different language combinations, and other methods. But it has contributed to challenging accepted truths in interpreting, and that is what is important in research, that is how we move the boundaries.

Lastly, do you have a growth plan? If so, what is it and who do you have to keep you accountable?

To be quite honest, no, not any more when it comes to interpreting. I'm suffering from the unbendable 24-hour condition. The day only has 24 hours and with teaching, research, and family, I have to put limits in order to survive. One of the decisions I had to make was to not try and become an expert interpreter. I have never considered myself to be an expert interpreter, and I will surely not become one now. Unfortunately, when I was 100 per cent active as interpreter, I wasn't aware of all the things I could do to improve. What I did was: 1) voice training, 2) recording myself *and* listening to it, and 3) interpreting at home from TV or radio (before the big Internet breakthrough). What I wish I had done (other than learning Dutch): 1) kept a working diary, 2) asked a colleague to be my mentor and scheduled practice sessions without a goal to pass a test or add a language, just with the goal to improve skills (e.g. sim with text, dealing with read speeches, how to deal with stress in the voice), and 3) started a community of practice.

Nowadays, I enjoy doing challenges with my students. When I give them a task to complete over a certain amount of time, I do the same task myself so that we can exchange real experiences, and they do not simply report to me what they did. That's a way to be accountable and it gives more nerve to the classes. They keep me accountable, and it's a great experience when the learning is shared between students and teacher.

Key chapter concepts

- There is something about having a Master's degree that makes it more difficult to admit that you need help.
- Doctors spend time training under other doctors, musicians work with teachers and conductors, sports people pay crazy sums for coaching. Interpreters nab a few YouTube videos and a term list and call it done.
- If interpreting is to go from a cost item to a value-added service, we will need to tackle our own fear of growth.
- If the future development and even survival of interpreting has an enemy, it is stagnation.

- There's so much more to expertise than just spending 10,000 hours on task.

Putting it into practice

Questions to ask

How easy do you find it to ask for help with your development as an interpreter?

How important do you think it is for your own growth to find a mentor or a coach?

In what areas of your professional and business practice do you think you may have stagnated? In which areas are you growing?

This chapter argues that we all need a growth plan, so that we set directions and goals for our development. Do you agree with this idea?

Actions to take

On your own

By now you probably can guess what I am going to ask you to do. First identify three areas of your professional and business practice. You might want to pick marketing, or sales, or technique in one or more interpreting modes, or your public speaking or any other areas. Once you have chosen these three areas, decide which is the most important and urgent of the three.

For the next three months, concentrate on this single area. Plan training activities, attend in person or virtual courses, read books, adjust your schedule around it. After you have done that for three months, review your progress.

When you review your progress, look at how you have grown and where still needs work. At this point, you may wish to concentrate on the next of your three areas or spend more time on the same part of your work. The key is to make regular, perceptible progress.

In a group

Now is the time to do perhaps the toughest challenge in the entire book. Pick a fellow interpreter who is particularly good at an area where you need to develop. Ask them to hold you accountable for your development in that area. It could simply be a monthly email check-in or a weekly Skype call to check your progress. Explain to them that you would like their help to direct your development. If they ask for payment, be ready to pay. It will be worth it in the end.

For larger groups of interpreters, setting up those kinds of mentoring relationships is absolutely vital. In fact, without such relationships, the impact of other CPD events could decrease. The challenge for us all is nothing short of total cultural change. Together, let's build a culture where interpreters take guided, deliberate development seriously and see it as part of our professionalism.

Notes

1 Elisabet Tiselius, 'Experience and Expertise in Conference Interpreting: An Investigation of Swedish Conference Interpreters' (University of Bergen, 2012), is a great start.
2 Elisabet Tiselius, 'Peak Performance for Interpreters: Practice Right', *eCPD Webinars*. Retrieved from www.ecpdwebinars.co.uk/downloads/performance-for-interpreters.
3 Don VandeWalle *et al.*, 'The Influence of Goal Orientation and Self-Regulation Tactics on Sales Performance: A Longitudinal Field Test', *Journal of Applied Psychology, 84*, no. 2 (1999): 249.
4 Tiselius, 'Experience and Expertise in Conference Interpreting: An Investigation of Swedish Conference Interpreters'.
5 K. Anders Ericsson *et al.*, *The Cambridge Handbook of Expertise and Expert Performance* (Cambridge University Press, 2006).
6 www.facebook.com/groups/607113549393499.

Chapter 4

Changing our public face
Branding, promotion, and public relations

Chapter summary

This chapter covers:

- The problem with selling our services as neutral and accurate,
- The messages that work for clients,
- The importance of selling interpreting on the basis of value, rather than necessity.

By now, one message should be clear. If interpreting is to thrive, we need to put adding value to clients at the centre of everything we do, from training and CPD to our approach to work and ethical decision making. Even doing that is not enough, however, if we keep talking about interpreting and selling it to clients in the same way we have been. As part of our overall quest to add value to our clients and profession, we need to adjust how we sell interpreting, too. To understand how that might work, it helps to get a feel for exactly what messages we are using now and what effect they are having. For that, I'd like to tell you a story.

In February 2015, I did something particularly crazy. I took a return journey of over six hours (actually nearer eight if you count train delays) for a one-hour lecture. The reason for my enthusiasm was purely the proven excellence of the speaker. Professor Ebru Diriker works in Turkey[1]. She has spent the last ten or so years investigating what clients want from interpreters, and, most importantly for this chapter, how interpreters have been selling their own profession.

Quite simply, her book, *De-/Re-Contextualising Conference Interpreting: Interpreters in the Ivory Tower?*, should be required reading for all interpreters, especially Chapters 2 and 3. In those two chapters, she comprehensively analyses what Turkish and international interpreting associations and Turkish interpreters have said about their profession. For many of us, the results are sadly predictable.

It seems that interpreters, or at least conference interpreters, are happy to talk about themselves in the same terms they have been for more than fifty years. Interpreters say they are neutral and impartial, don't get involved, are accurate as to what the speaker meant (or intended!), and never add or omit anything. In short, they are language machines on legs, dictionaries with a caffeine habit, Google Translate in a suit.

It wouldn't be quite so bad if any of that were actually true. Interpreters know, even if they don't like to admit it, that neutrality is problematic, additions and omissions are often necessary, and no two people actually agree on what 'accuracy' is. At best, they are presenting clients with a picture of what 'ideal' interpreting would look like. It isn't and can't ever be the interpreting they deliver. Interpreters are human after all.

Ironically, the most important problem for interpreting today, therefore, is that the image interpreters have worked so hard to cultivate doesn't actually reflect what they do. The issue goes much deeper, though. In the Introduction, I explored the idea that businesses always find room in the budget for priorities. With that in mind, the biggest issue for the future of interpreting isn't pay or conditions or technology, but *value*. The greatest priority for every interpreter and every interpreting association is to convince potential clients that their services are valuable.

It is difficult to do that within traditional boundaries. If interpreters try to stand on the unsteady ground of neutrality and accuracy, they shouldn't really be surprised when clients take those ideas to their logical conclusion. If we view ourselves as not much more than Google Translate in a suit, why wouldn't clients use machine interpreting of some form? If processing language is the majority of our work, then it makes sense to find the cheapest, fastest language processors around: computers.

To put it another way, when we sell interpreting on the basis of accuracy, even though it is vital, we are like a used-car salesman crowing about the fact that every car he sells has a working engine. Well, yes, of course they have working engines. One would expect nothing less. The mere fact of having a functional engine just means the car will go. It isn't exactly a unique selling point.

Accuracy is something that clients will take for granted. That will not change, no matter how much we try to convince them that it is not as easy as they might think.

Remote interpreting is also hard to argue against within our traditional boundaries. We can argue all we like about sight lines, concentration, and stress, but if our presence in the room is for no other reason than possibly elevated levels of stress then I doubt most clients will care.

For interpreting to thrive, we need an entirely new approach. Unsurprisingly, I am going to continue to argue that value should be at the crux of this new approach. Let me explain.

I recently got into an interesting email conversation with a colleague. What is more important than the conversation itself is that throughout it, I couldn't help but notice her email signature that said, "83 per cent of buyers are more likely to choose your product if I provide content". I don't know how she procured that figure, but it and her statement are worth dissecting a bit.

Firstly, her claim is incredibly specific. She makes a strong claim and gives an actual number. There is none of the typical 'interpreters are accurate' drivel.

Instead, she claims to make a measurable impact, expressed in terms clients care about. What client doesn't want to be more likely to be chosen?

Secondly, her claim doesn't mention translation or interpreting. That might seem counterintuitive, but it is actually very clever. Clients may well have preconceived ideas of what our work is about. This colleague made a deliberate decision to bypass those preconceived notions and promote her services in terms that are associated with adding value rather than using blithe terms like 'translation' or 'interpreting'.

Lastly, the undeniable message behind all of this is not that she is accurate or neutral, but that her services make a marked difference. She states unequivocally that clients will have more success working with her than trying to do things on their own. 'Come to me', she says, 'and I will make your company better, more profitable, more likely to be chosen'. What a statement!

All aspects of that hook add up to savvy marketing and PR, without a hint of our traditional, staid sales pitches. It is this type of creative PR that our industry so desperately needs. If interpreting is to move from being a cost item to being seen a worthwhile investment, interpreters need to build stories and evidence of why an event or appointment or court case will function better, work more effectively, or make more money with interpreters than without them. In fact, interpreters might even need to help people see that a multilingual meeting is always better than a monolingual one.

In short, we need to move from seeing and selling interpreting as all about filling a need into seeing and selling interpreting as an integral service that adds value. Our clients need to be convinced that the returns they will get from excellent interpreting will far outweigh the admittedly rather high costs they will need to pay. Interpreters might not be cheap, but our clients are worth it.

Before we even get to that stage, though, we need to convince ourselves. Do we really believe we make a difference? Can we think of stories where our work produced tangible results? Could we find clients who will back us up?

Here is where it becomes obvious that interpreting and interpreters need a re-branding exercise. Instead of being so invisible that we perform ourselves out of a job, we need to be so valuable that we become impossible to replace. Take the wood-industry job I mentioned in Chapter 1. In discussions, I found out that they had had previous problems with interpreters. Most of their complaints pointed to inadequate preparation, but the positive feedback they gave to me pointed to the creation of value. They wanted to work with me because I helped them achieve their goals.

Is it just possible that when people become convinced that interpreting helps them achieve their goals, most of interpreter issues with pay and conditions might shrink or even disappear altogether? What we need then is to build up real-life cases, with the permission of our clients, which demonstrate just how we have added value and helped them. 'Mr Downie is an excellent interpreter' is good; 'we sold 50 per cent more with Mr Downie and his team at the conference' is considerably better.

For some interpreters, this might seem somewhat suspect. After all, some of us work in court or medical interpreting where making sales (and money) isn't the goal. If money isn't the goal, we need to know what is. It needs to be we help create value for clients in helping them achieve what they want to achieve or helping an event – whether it's a court case, doctor's appointment, university lecture, or political conference – run successfully.

If one works in court, the obvious goal is justice. Imagine the difference it would make if judges were to write to the national government and say, "Trials go much better and the results are much fairer with Mr/Ms X on the team". What if they wrote "We can trust that when we use a professional interpreter, the outcome will be fair. He (or she) not only helps us communicate, he or she helps us understand". That's added value and it can be argued that it saves money in the longer term, too.

As a strategy, the idea being seen to add value rather than a cost item is much more effective than protesting against cost cutting. If we are to get the right kind of PR, we need to be able to articulate why hiring professional interpreters results in best practices in terms that make sense to those who decide if there is room in the budget. Can we state, honestly, that using professionals actually contributes to *lower* costs in the medium and longer term? Can we demonstrate that people are more likely to get better medical treatment on the first visit, so doctors and patients don't waste time and money on subsequent visits?

So, if this book is about adding value to our clients and our profession, the way we talk about and sell interpreting must centre on one key message: interpreting helps people achieve what they want to achieve (and perhaps even more!). Everything I have said about research on client expectations, the whole discussion about email signatures and tangible results, the need to question what seem to be the values of our profession: they all add up to that single idea.

We need to rebrand. We need to prove wrong the voices that see interpreting as a cost item by taking hold of our own image and PR. We need to purposefully and carefully present the facts about how professional interpreting creates more value than it costs. We need to resist the temptation to protest cost-item status and replace it with affirmation of the good interpreting does and the positive effect interpreters each have on events and those we work with.

It isn't a good idea to look to the regulated professions, such as lawyers and doctors, for an example of how to achieve this. A more relevant comparison would be with professions where value creation is deemed to be part of the package, such as business and management consultants. Anyone with the time and inclination can set themselves up as some form of consultant and attempt to get work.

Their business model might resemble that of interpreting, but a big difference is that management consultants realised a long time ago that the only way they would be able to get the kinds of fees they wanted was to show clearly how they add value. After all, it is entirely possible to run a business and never use the services of a consultant. If they were going to convince people to hire them, they needed to show that it was worth it. Interpreters have yet to achieve that.

As overwhelming as rebranding an entire profession might seem, it is possible if we view it in terms of rebranding our own individual work. We can and should care about details such as business cards, client testimonials, marketing plans, and business names. It absolutely matters that clients can see in us the potential to reach or even exceed their goals. For these types of tasks, we need a guide. There is no better guide to branding, marketing, and PR for interpreters than Valeria Aliperta. I am really pleased to be able to interview her for this chapter.

Interview with Valeria Aliperta

You are known as an expert on branding for translators and interpreters. What first piqued your interest in that topic?

Passion is something you are born with. With my curiosity for everything new and aesthetically pleasant, with a detour via art and design plus input from my other half who is a designer, well. . . . I ended up reading and learning more and more on branding. So, to answer your question, I found myself in it naturally: following people's kind comments on how nice my logo identity was and how clear my brand and style was, I started being asked how they could do it, too, and if I could help them. So I did.

What do you think are the key elements of a successful interpreting brand?

To my mind, the major elements are:

*   *Visual clarity* – Think of the biggest brands around you. They become familiar and known to everyone, and most of the time – if not all – the thing they share is clarity of design, clearly recognisable and clean. That's important for a successful brand, because it is something people easily remember and can trust.
*   *Clever concept* – It has to has something that one does not immediately perceive, or one does, but it still strikes you as clever. My own brand (Rainy London Translations) is fairly obvious, but it encapsulates a mix of factual reality (London is rainy, and we all know that) and a bit of wittiness (it's a funny name, being that you would not expect it for a business like mine). This causes a giggle in most people, but it also brings about the guarantee that they will certainly remember it. And the name has 'London' in it, so online geo-referenced searches are easily directed to my page/profile.
*   *Timeless yet innovative* – The challenge for any brand, and especially for those in a very specific industry like ours, is to 'be an evergreen', yet stand out for the innovative approach or different spin on things. The use of minimal lines and colours is key in my experience, and makes for staying power – my logo is almost seven years old and it still is relevant.

Branding is also about an overall vision for your business. This can be created with a bit of strategic planning. Once you know the 'what' of your business (your services or product), the main elements for you to consider are:

- *Where:* where do you want to get with this? In other words, locate your objectives, identify your clients, and evaluate where you stand in the market and where you see your business going in the future.
- *When:* how long do you envisage this will take? What is the time deadline you set for yourself to achieve your goal? Is it a SMART goal? Is it feasible and viable in such a timeline?
- *Why:* why are you doing this? What do you want to achieve with it? By determining why you do it, you can also define very clearly and quickly what your edge is, and what is the unique selling position (USP) that differentiates you from the rest of your competitors.
- *Who (brand voice):* who or what is the defining voice or spirit of your brand? To whom are you talking; who is your audience? What tone of voice and style should your brand have, consistently? Who is the ideal customer and how does he or she behave? What would your audience expect you to say and how?

Follow contemplation of those 'Wh' questions with considering some basic brand guidelines, such as: what do I write in an email? Do I invoice in hard copy or only in e-format? Do I need to be present on social media? If so, which one? Branding guidelines can be about anything you need for your business. They are the instructions you abide by to ensure that your business stays true to who you are all the time. People trust *consistency* and *genuine behaviours*. It's about being a defined brand, being 'predictable' in the way you would do or say something. If you are, it means your brand is recognisable and really has a style that nobody will ever confuse with another.

How important do you think colour and name choice is for brand building? Can you tell us the story behind your name and colour choice?

Incredibly important! I recommend sticking to the three Vs: visible, versatile, and vibrant. Colour is the element that is generally seen as the easiest to choose, at least from a design point of view, yet considering the chromatic power of colour is crucial to making sure the right message comes across to the right prospects. Start by knowing for certain what palette you like and what you do not. Here are a few tips to choosing a colour or colour scheme:

- *Start from what you know and like.* Ultimately, you are your number one customer and critical consumer, so trust that you know best.
- *Be open.* Ask others, bear in mind gender and demographics, and see where it leads you. If everyone you ask gives you the same perception of a specific shade or shades, reconsider.

- *Research your competitors' choices.* Did they use the same colour(s)? Is anyone standing out? Why?
- *Consider cultural issues.* Analyse/assess your cultural references and those of your target countries. Maybe red means something to or is associated with a specific concept in India but not in Europe, and so on.
- *Keep it simple.* Don't put too much strain on the eye, but do achieve your purpose. Attracting attention is one thing, affecting your audience's retinas is a no-no.
- *Think about consumers.* Explore what you want your customers to feel. Maybe you'll see that a specific group of customers or target demographic prefers one specific colour you didn't even consider before.
- *Be aware of the digital versus real-life world.* Consider how colours transition from physical to digital worlds and vice versa, and the different looks they can have in different media. Every shade looks paler or darker in print, and brighter or sometimes completely different on screen.
- *Go back to basics.* Think of times prior to the advent of colour in marketing media. Consider black and white. Do those work? Those are colours, too!
- *Defy the diktat.* Don't be constrained by 'the fashion of the moment'. Who said men cannot wear pink?
- *Don't be afraid to change.* They say, 'If it ain't broken, don't fix it', but still, why can't you change a colour or rebrand after a while? They also say, 'Only diamonds are forever'!

Rainy London Translations was an easy choice for me. I love black – as a matter of fact, my latest project has a black and white design (www.thestylishfreelancer. com), but back then I wanted something less aggressive. I like red, too, so I opted for brick red and blue. The shades are used along with white – a third colour I always recommend you consider because it gives new life to your design when use it in combination with another shade. Rainy London Translations' palette recreated the colours of the Union Jack, the flag of the United Kingdom; the red has slightly evolved toward a pillar-box red over the years, yet remaining true to the initial concept.

Are there any marketing or branding faux pas that you think we need to avoid?

I can recommend three Don'ts and three Dos:

- DO NOT use too many colours in your brand/logo.
- DO NOT underestimate other people's opinions.
- DO NOT use a channel you're not comfortable with just because everybody else is.
- DO create a strategy and a brand voice.
- DO perform some research on competitors and trends of your industry, and do know your limits.

- DO hire a professional for design, copy, and other components that are not part of your core business (i.e. just do what YOU are good at).

How do you think we can rebrand interpreting to show how valuable it is?

Certainly a very good question, Jonathan. I always try to raise awareness among my clients to educate them on why in the booth you need two people and not one. I believe it could start with books like this and blogs or even podcasts that explain what an interpreter really does, and go on with seminars and activities like the one I recently had the honour to be part of in a local school. In March 2015, I was invited to talk to groups of pupils between 14 and 16 years of age about interpreting: I approached it in practical terms, explaining what we do, how and why, explaining the importance of being open minded and getting to know cultures. We also tried practice activities to make sure the students experienced the process 'live', realised how challenging this discipline can be and how skilled you need to be to do a great job that really makes a difference. Interpreters could also look into creating a clear, innovative design and brand that we could all use as a category to be recognised for the essential role we play for society and economies.

Can you think of an interpreting assignment where you made an obvious difference for your clients?

Of course I have to mention the countless occasions in a hospital or a court environment, where I interpreted for people getting treatment or help – that certainly makes you feel good and really useful to society. Yet, my favourite part is the sensation after a deal goes well and the parties shake hands after a meeting; or when a plenary conference gets to the conclusion and the host thanks the interpreters for their brilliant job. Without us, all these events, all this communication, would never be possible – at least in a successful way. We are the lever that makes the world go round, really – and sometimes I feel we are not recognised for that at all.

I noticed that your website includes client testimonials. How easy were they to get?

In my experience, it was quite a straightforward process: happy client, happy email or phone call, ideal moment to ask for a few lines of praise. They normally tend to compliment me or drop me a line to say they are very happy with the work without me asking, and the best part of this is when they talk about you to others and you get work referral work. I'd say it's quite a common practice now to get LinkedIn testimonials, too, and most people are happy to help. The main thing to bear in mind is to always ask them for permission, as privacy laws – and people's sensitivity – do vary from country to country.

What books or articles do you think interpreters should read to help them get a handle on marketing, PR, and branding?

I rarely have time to read chunky volumes these days, and I tend to read a lot for preparation work and less and less for pleasure, alas; I love reading. I blame that on the avalanche of info I digest via social media, and the serious lack of holidays I tend to take! But when I can read I do like marketing-related books or short essays. Still, I can wholeheartedly recommend the following short selection of recent reads:

- *Rework* by Jason Fried and David Heinemeier Hansson. This book will change the way you work forever. Just read it.
- *Vivere altrove* by Marisa Fenoglio. It's a novel, it's in Italian, but it simply talks about life away from your country, getting to know a new world in a new language. Simply amazing literature that really opens your eyes on the 'other'.
- *Ogilvy on Advertising or Confessions of an Advertising Man* by David Ogilvy. Simple theories and candid ideas from the father of modern advertising.
- *How to Be a Graphic Designer without Losing Your Soul* by Adrian Shaughnessy. Apply this to anything. Simple guidelines to build a business in the right way.
- Anything from my branding blog rainylondonbranding.com or my style platform thestylishfreelancer.com.

Key chapter concepts

- The biggest issue for the future of interpreting isn't pay or conditions or technology, but *value*.
- If processing language is the majority of our work then it makes sense to find the cheapest, fastest language processors around: computers.
- Accuracy is something that clients will take for granted.
- We need to resist the temptation to protest cost-item status and replace it with affirmation of the good interpreting does.
- We are the lever that makes the world go round.

Putting it into practice

Questions to ask

How much time and effort do you put into your personal brand and the way you come across to prospective clients?

Why do you think your clients chose you above other interpreters? Why might new clients choose you?

In your marketing efforts, are you more like the used-car salesman, crowing about having a functional engine, or the management consultant, selling value?

Do you agree that interpreting needs a rebrand?

Actions to take

On your own

Take an honest look at your website and business cards. What do they say about your business? What would you like them to say?

Starting with one aspect of your business brand, make a list of how you would like it to change and approach a designer to get an estimate of how much a rebrand would cost.

Redraft the copy on your website and public profiles to emphasise the value you add to clients.

Poll some of your most recent clients to see what they look for in an interpreter and what they think of the services you offer.

In a group

We can only rebrand interpreting by working together. Working with either a group of colleagues you know well or in consultation with your local professional association, compile stories of how interpreters add value and start a blog containing them.

Notes

1 You will hear more from her in Chapter 7.

Chapter 5

Guilds, information hubs, or communities of practice?

Working with professional associations

Chapter summary

This chapter covers:

- The importance of professional associations,
- Why creating legal protection will never be enough,
- Three keys to the future success of professional associations.

A strong profession needs strong professional associations. While it is true that only a small percentage of interpreters will play a lead role in the organisations that cover our profession, every interpreter has a stake in how professional associations work and the roles they play. As much as we might like to think of ourselves as independent and self-sufficient, the truth is that our prestige, place, and power are all direct results of the work we do as a community.

Professional associations are one of the most effective ways we can work together. While this chapter mentions the benefits of being part of more informal professional communities like those on Facebook or LinkedIn, or small informal in-person groups, there simply is no replacement for a high-quality, well-run professional association. Joining a professional association is key to ensuring that we add value to our clients and to our professions. If we are to grow as interpreters, we need the power of professional associations to work for us and with us.

In the Introduction, I mentioned that in most cases, the challenges faced by interpreters can only be fully tackled at both the individual and group levels. At the individual level, we work on our skills, ensure we always deliver high-quality services, and operate with the skilful efficiency of a high-class business. At the group level, we lobby, illustrate how interpreting creates value, carry out research, and set standards. One level cannot exist without the other. Professional interpreting cannot survive without a focus on both individual and group work.

While it might seem that strengthening professional associations and positioning them for the future is something that can only be done as a group, there are some significant individual actions that are required, too. These individual actions have a direct effect on the status of our profession – something that none of us can afford to ignore. But before we get there, I need to discuss what is meant by a 'professional association'. On this point, I am indebted to Anthony Pym[1].

He points out that the shape and purpose of professional associations for translators and interpreters have changed over time. Whereas many of the oldest associations started at a time when the top priority seemed to be guarding the status and rates of these nascent professions, newer associations have preferred to act as communities.

The earlier associations, which seemed to work hierarchically and attempted to act as gatekeepers, required that people had to attain a certain level of experience or performance to be able to join. Once they were in, there was an acceptance that communication would be mostly unidirectional, that information and expertise would flow from the upper-end of the hierarchy – the presidents and committee heads – to the rest of the members and then to the outside world. Joining such associations was therefore seen as the 'gold standard' of professionalism, signalling to clients that this person was worth working with. It was 'gilt by association', if you will pardon the pun.

Newer associations, however, have tended to reject this model, not least because it is becoming increasingly difficult to act as gatekeepers in a world where online job portals decentralise the process of finding interpreters and where associations face legal challenges every time they try to set or recommend rates. What's more, with the rise of social media, people have grown used to communicating on an equal footing with anyone, whether they are leaders of major corporations or a next door neighbour. It is little wonder then that it has become more common for groups of interpreters or translators to self-organise on a less-formal footing, creating groups based on locality or interest, constructing teams and using social media to allow two-way or multi-way communication.

In short, what professionals seem to want is a community of practice, not a closed shop. Here, however, is where I would like to take things further than Anthony does. While he, quite rightly, argues that professional associations will need to continue to prove the value of their current forms while helping to create communities of practice, I think there is much more to it than that. Quite simply, the future of interpreting associations will involve finding ways to encourage their members to add value to clients. To do that, they will need three attributes: humility, decentralisation, and connection. To explain these, we first need to rethink why we need professional associations at all.

If we imagine, as many older professional associations did, that the purpose of an association is to restrict access to the profession, then what we essentially have is a guild. The purpose of a guild is to look after the interests of a profession by deliberately making those skills scarce and therefore forcing clients to using a guild member. If you lived in medieval York and you wanted a new pitchfork, you would find that the only people allowed to make one for you were the members of a local craft guild. Since being part of the guild meant not undercutting your fellow craftspeople, you would find that prices were mostly consistent throughout the entire town.

Here, no one particularly cares about the interest of the farmers who actually need a pitchfork. It's a case of 'get it here or do without.' There are some interpreters who would very much like a similar system for our profession today. Instead of working hard to add value to clients, the running theme in their discussions is how they can restrict clients and pull strings to create some kind of legal system that means that their group, the people they like, will get all the work. As unreasonable as this might seem, there are good historical reasons why such tactics have never really gone away.

In the early days, when interpreting was being formalised in response to the rise in international organisations, it seemed a really good idea that interpreters, who belonged to a small and new profession with no real recognition, should ensure that none of their mates got short-changed by making sure that everyone charged similar rates and offered similar services. Since interpreting seemed pretty difficult, too, the idea of standard conditions arose.

For a new, fairly unknown profession without any sort of historical heritage (although that heritage would soon be rediscovered), this seemed reasonable. The powerful forces of market economics would seem to be set against small professions like (conference) interpreting, since they had no real status or track record to use as a leveraging tool. In short, no one was looking out for interpreters, so they had to look out for themselves.

The emphasis in that world was, therefore, in giving interpreting a much-needed foothold and then making sure that new interpreters understood what had been achieved and didn't let things slip. However, what was good for clients was never really considered. Quite simply, there was too much else going on.

An even simpler argument as to why the needs and requirements of clients would not be the focus of any real reflection until the late 1980s, nearly forty years after the first interpreting associations burst onto the scene, was that professional interpreters tended to work with clients who were already powerful. Diplomats, politicians, and international lawyers seemed to be doing pretty well and were used to having things their own way. The role of an interpreting association could, therefore, be viewed as an attempt to ensure that interpreters got some means of control and power and were not taken advantage of by their powerful clients.

With powerful clients, a short history, a restricted market, and limited numbers, the guild model was at that time what interpreting probably needed. Once interpreters started to attempt to make the guild model work with different forms of interpreting, uncontrolled markets, and a globalised world, however, strains began to show. Creating a guild that regulates and restricts interpreting in any situation, anywhere in the world was impossible, as well as ill advised, it turns out.

It is also ethically questionable to assume that the guild model is valid when interpreters work in situations with massive imbalances of power. There is logic behind people who are new to a country wanting a friend or family member to interpret for them at the first visit to the doctor or to help them with their first attempt at getting a house. We can make the case on the basis of good research[2] that professional interpreters tend to deliver a more competent service than a friend or family member would, but the moment we insist that professionals always be used, we run the risk adding to the feeling of powerlessness among some clients. We might also be ignoring the reasons why they might trust family members more than outsiders in some sensitive cases. In wanting to ensure that people get access to the best quality of interpreting, we need to make sure we still allow them a measure of power to make key decisions themselves.

If we are expecting professional associations to act as gatekeepers and want our membership fees to be tantamount to tolls, we are missing the point. What we need is not legal protection, but community – not a castle with a drawbridge, but something more akin to a business incubator and support network.

Some might point to forms of interpreting that still have the same elements as early conference interpreting and might seem to need the same kind of protection. Court interpreters could, for instance, argue that they often work for lawyers (powerful clients), have a short history as a recognised profession, and limited numbers. Might the guild model work for them?

This is where it gets complicated. There are strong arguments for limiting who can be an interpreter in certain contexts, but those arguments mostly rest on the risk of something going horribly wrong. We almost always argue for protection for medical interpreters or court interpreters since we know that their work can really be a matter of life and death, liberty, or custody. Even in these cases, however, the most we can ever do is try to stipulate the qualifications or standards that interpreters have to meet. As beneficial as that tactic might seem, all such standards can ever do is measure how an individual performed at a given moment in time and whether he or she can convince people that such a performance will be maintained.

No standards or requirements, no matter how stringent, can guarantee that interpreters will perform excellently every time. All they can do is to create a system of checks and safeguards that reduce the likelihood of mistakes and provide a way of resolving any problems that might come up. There will never be enough money to monitor every interpreting job, even in a single setting like courts or hospitals.

Even in the best possible world, we would need something in addition to any requirements or barriers to entry that we might want to create. What we need is a set of community-wide values that helps interpreters understand what it means to be an interpreter, wherever they might work. Instead of taking what seemed like good values for conference interpreting and applying them blindly to every other setting, we need to find the common denominator for all forms of interpreting and then make that the foundation for all the work we do.

As I have argued repeatedly throughout the book, that foundation, that common denominator, is adding value. A court interpreter adds value by applying his or her skills, knowledge, and experience to help ensure justice is done. A medical interpreter adds value by acting intelligently to ensure that medical diagnoses and treatments are carried out sensitively and effectively, no matter the linguistic or cultural barriers. A sports interpreter adds value by creating texts that journalists can use to inform. If professional associations can do anything, they can build this sense of community – *common unity* around the purpose of using the power and privilege we have in a responsible, value-adding way. By moving the focus from how we can force clients to do things and onto how we can help them achieve things, we build a much stronger case for precisely the improvements in status, power, and (of course!) rates, that we want.

Returning to the case of someone wanting a family member to interpret for them in some cases, it might make more sense to help people understand how a professional interpreter could be of more help, be more valuable, than a family member, rather than simply imposing rules that take the decision out of their hands. Conversely, the more we work together in our professional associations to help those who hold the power understand how interpreters help them do their jobs more effectively, the more they are likely to promote the use of professionals, too.

If we want to add value to our clients and our profession, we need to all play our part in building the kind of community that promotes the common values of all forms of interpreting. As stated previously, we need to take an avid interest in how interpreters are trained and how we develop ourselves. In this chapter, the focus is on interpreters taking an interest in the communities we are part of and how they can be kept healthy. Part of that health will always be an outward – or value – focus, rather than operating from a defensive position, trying desperately to hold onto our patch.

With that in mind, we come back to the need for humility, decentralisation, and connection. Our need for humility derives directly from the obvious problems with the guild model. The guild model's survival relies on us convincing clients that the standards and requirements we might want to set are relevant to their needs. If we push that too forcefully without taking into consideration their individual needs and how best to serve those, we come across as bullies trying to get our way. The more we are seen as dictating to clients whom they should work with, the more likely clients are to resist. The more we attempt to force them to view us more highly, the less willing they are to do so, if for no other reason than the fact that we still need to persuade them that it is always in their interest to use proper professionals.

Humility, therefore, starts with realising that we are not yet at the stage that people see interpreting of any kind as being on a par with being a lawyer, a doctor, or even an engineer. We still have a long way to go to convince people that we provide that level of value to society. We must begin by admitting that we have a better impression of our own work than most of our clients have. Our protestations and standardizations won't make governments want to protect interpreting, and that isn't likely to change. Operating with humility also means accepting that there are some situations in which clients would rather use their friends or family members, and that such decisions are not always about saving money.

Humility means admitting all that, but also not lying down in defeat or falling into whining or navel-gazing. Instead, it means starting from where we are and looking around to see what we might do in the meantime to demonstrate how much value we actually bring. We can shamelessly acknowledge that we aren't lawyers while simultaneously showing how we help lawyers do their work. We can freely admit that we aren't doctors while giving examples of patients who could not have been treated unless we were there. Perhaps humility means being in awe of the power of interpreting and working to give others that same sense of awe.

Humility just might mean letting go of our feelings of superiority and working to find solutions that add value to both our profession and our clients. Taking court interpreting as an example: humility might mean arguing not that interpreting should be legally protected but that courts need reliable ways of ensuring the quality of the interpreting they receive. Interpreters and their professional associations could quite happily work with courts to figure out systems and marks that make sense to them and correspond to their needs.

Professional associations, therefore, need to gain humility to realise that the old models of working need to be rethought, and that clients need to contribute to the establishment of a new model. Associations need humility to realise that much of interpreters' work over the foreseeable future should focus on persuading people who currently have no interest in interpreting that it matters to them.

Part of this humility will involve decentralisation. Here again, we come up against the traditional hierarchical model, where communication comes from the top to the bottom, and insubordination is not tolerated. Today, as people grow comfortable with the idea of having a tweet read by a CEO or prime minister, they are less likely to accept that belonging to a professional association means belonging to an exclusive club where only a few voices can be heard.

Even a cursory glance at the growth of interpreting groups on Facebook will tell you that interpreters are looking to join networked communities. We want to feel that we are not on our own. We want to be able to ask questions and help others. We want to share resources and ideas freely.

As time goes on, the pressure will increase for professional associations to provide spaces for sharing to happen or risk becoming irrelevant. Gone are the days when poring over the minutiae of organisational bylaws were seen as a marker of commitment to your profession, if those days ever existed in the first place! Instead, we are discovering that knowledge is for sharing and the precise structure of an organisation is far less important than the quality of community it creates.

The idea of creating community leads inexorably to the need for connection. 'Connection' to me means much more than just getting someone to click a link on LinkedIn or hit 'follow' on Twitter. Connection means being ready to knock over the typical barriers and bring together clients, freelancers, staffers, conference interpreters, sign language interpreters, medical interpreters, court interpreters, government officials, and anyone, in fact, who has an interest in producing or receiving high-quality interpreting.

That type of connectivity helps us as a profession gain a better hearing from other professionals by allowing us to speak from the position of representing an entire industry rather than one particular section of it. There may well be places where having some sort of protection or required certification of interpreters might be necessary, but it will be much easier for that to receive government approval when clients and interpreters alike are clamouring for it. Actually, if both clients and interpreters agreed on the requirements that needed to be set, legal protection might be unnecessary anyway!

My point is that it is only by accepting the current state of play before working to change it, building supportive communities, and working actively across the barriers we have artificially erected, that professional associations can hope to prove that they are worthwhile. And it is only by playing our individual parts in this work that we can ever hope to add value to clients sustainably. It is difficult to see how any group except a well-organised professional association could manage to reconcile the need to support interpreters and improve their status with the need to encourage them to add value to their clients. As good as Facebook groups can be, you need a structured, formal organisation to turn community into change and one-off successes into long-term partnership.

As daunting as all this work might seem and as much as it obviously requires real coordination among large groups of interpreters, individual interpreters have to participate as well. If we want professional associations that have the power to bring change, they need our effort and input. We can complain all we like about conditions, but it is only when we actively work with our national and international professional associations that change becomes realistic. A few hours volunteering at a language fair, a few pages of an article, a few days' worth of work mentoring or serving on a committee: all these 'fews' add up. As someone who has served on the board of a national association, I know that the strength of any association is not found in its bank account but in the commitment of its members. If we want the future to be different than the present, it is our time and energy that we will need to dedicate to helping it happen. It's time to stop complaining and start working.

There are few people better placed to explain the power of an association that represents the entire industry than Iwan Davies, Chair of the Institute of Translation and Interpreting (ITI), the UK's premier association for the translation and interpreting industries, from 2013 to 2016. As he explains in the interview, ITI brings together all those with an interest in our professions, including clients. It's the united model espoused by ITI that will become increasingly necessary in future.

Interview with Iwan Davies

Iwan, you have been at the heart of the United Kingdom's largest professional organisation for the translation and interpreting professions for some time now. Could you explain what first made you want to get involved?

I've been a member of ITI since 1999, and first got involved as a regional group committee member in 2001, and then as a committee member at the national level in 2006. Before volunteering, while I found that my experience as a member gave me plenty in the way of information when I didn't always understand the background, and I also felt that there was something missing in my relationship with the profession and the professional association. I suppose I came to see my relationship with ITI as needing to be two-way – giving me the opportunity to put time back in, but also allowing me to help shape the decisions that would allow the Institute to grow and the profession to thrive.

How do you think the work of ITI has changed over the past few years? What is ITI doing more of or less of?

Fundamentally, ITI's work has always had the aim of creating a platform on which all parts of the translation and interpreting professions can stand together to promote what we do, and I don't think that has changed at all. Naturally, the ways we deliver service to members and non-members have changed, as new opportunities have arisen, but ITI has always had a focus on the needs of those currently providing translation and interpreting services, those of future professionals, and those of translation and interpreting service users. We've been pretty consistent in our outreach to universities, for example, as well as in our approaches to businesses, especially exporters. Perhaps one area that we are developing more now is schools outreach, which is extremely important in view of the declining numbers of children studying languages.

ITI has members who are translators, interpreters, universities, and LSPs (Language Service Providers) of all varieties. Could you explain the rationale for having such a broad membership base and the impact that base has on the way ITI interacts with other stakeholders, such as government or the public?

One of ITI's founding members described it to me as follows: "ITI was deliberately set up as a 'broad church' association for anyone, or any organisation, that engages in any activity that would be classified as translation or interpreting. In the early days, these included the UK Foreign and Commonwealth Office; universities; large 'consumers', such as industrial multinationals; translation companies of all sorts, provided they met the criteria, which included references from ITI members; and, of course, individual practitioners (with a grey division between those who did it all themselves and those who 'sometimes' subcontracted – de facto neo-agencies in all but name, and even that was blurred as people had 'trading names' or even Ltd. company status)." The rationale was very much based on the aim I mentioned above, of creating a single platform for us all to use to stand together. Of course, there are inevitable frictions between some groups, but our diversity is our strength because it allows us to speak across the professions, rather than at narrow parts.

A key idea of this chapter and of the entire book is that real change needs both individual and group action. Could you explain a little about how individuals and groups contribute to the work of ITI?

Group action is most obvious when it comes to our networks and regional groups, which is where most of the volunteer time is spent nowadays. In these groups, practising translators and interpreters engage with communities of practice directly to effect change, whether that be through organisation of CPD, provision of social opportunities to lone freelancers, or outreach to consumers, future professionals, or other interested parties. At the individual level, the most marked development in recent years has been the professionalisation of the professions in respect to CPD – ITI has led the way in raising awareness of the need for professional translators and interpreters to constantly update their knowledge and skills, and our members contribute to the Institute's work through their involvement in the design and delivery of courses for new and experienced members alike.

Many interpreters are threatened by what seem to be constant attempts to drive down rates and force poorer conditions. What can individual interpreters do to help their profession thrive despite these challenges?

The most important thing that any professional can do to defend their professional status is to act professionally. That sounds simplistic, but what it really means is if you want to be taken seriously and you want your true worth to be appreciated in terms of the value you bring, you need to show the other professions that use your services that you contribute exactly the same effort, diligence, and professionalism as they do. Recently, interpreters have withheld their labour to demonstrate to service users what happens when professionals' work is not valued and non-professionals step in to fill the gaps. The results have not been pretty, and there are signs that service users are coming to understand. However, the process has been painful for all, and is not necessarily a strategy I would recommend. But the circumstances are fairly extraordinary. Normally, I feel that a cohesive stance of demonstrated professionalism is much more productive.

Finally, if you had to give one piece of advice for interpreters wondering how they could help grow and strengthen their professional association, what would it be?

When it comes to collective representation through a professional association, all professionals need to be able to see beyond their own requirements and understand the needs of the entire spectrum, from providers to consumers and from students to educators. The key aim has to be professional unity.

Key chapter concepts

- A strong profession needs strong professional associations.
- It is becoming increasingly difficult to act as gatekeepers in a world where online job portals decentralise the process of finding interpreters.
- The future of interpreting associations will involve three things: humility, decentralisation, and connection.
- What we need is a set of community-wide values that helps interpreters understand what it means to be an interpreter, wherever they might work.
- The most important thing that any professional can do to defend their professional status is to act professionally.

Putting it into practice

Questions to ask

What do you want from professional associations?

This chapter suggested that the guild model rarely, if ever, accomplishes what we want it to. How far do you agree with this?

What do you think the advantages are of having an association that can speak for everyone with an interest in interpreting? What might the disadvantages be?

How much of your time do you dedicate to helping the professional associations of which you are a member?

Actions to take

On your own

Investigate the needs of the professional associations of which you are a member and decide where you can best invest your time as a volunteer.

Look for Facebook or LinkedIn groups of fellow interpreters and join them. Compare the outcomes of their work with the work of a professional association.

In a group

Ask the necessary hard questions of your association. Is it ready for the future of interpreting? Does it speak for the whole industry or just one part of it? What more can you do to encourage professionalism and continued professional development?

Notes

1 Anthony Pym, 'Translator Associations—from Gatekeepers to Communities', *Target*, *26*, no. 3 (2014): 466–91.

2 Ellen Rosenberg, Yvan Leanza, and Robbyn Seller, 'Doctor–Patient Communication in Primary Care with an Interpreter: Physician Perceptions of Professional and Family Interpreters', *Patient Education and Counseling*, *67*, no. 3 (2007): 286–92.

Chapter 6

We're all in this together
Uniting our divided professions

Chapter summary

This chapter covers:

- Why interpreting tends to be divided,
- Why all interpreters need to unite and what happens when we don't,
- What interpreters in different settings can learn from each other.

There is no better place to go from discussing professional associations than to the need to unite interpreting as one cohesive unit. If you doubt the need for unity, let me remind you of a story.

It was after the passing of Nelson Mandela, and the world was in mourning. His memorial service was to be an international affair. The world's media were focused on the stage. Sharing that stage with hundreds of heads of state and dignitaries stood an 'interpreter' by the name of Thamsanqa Jantjie. Sadly for interpreting and for Deaf people in South Africa and the world over, Mr Jantjie would soon earn himself the label of 'fake interpreter' for his mix of repetition and aimless gesticulation. Whatever he was doing, it certainly wasn't sign-language interpreting.

As much as this incident tells us about the need for transparent and reliable hiring procedures for interpreters at such big, public occasions[1], it also tells us much about the status of our professions themselves. As startling as the 'Fake Interpreter' incident was, it is almost impossible to imagine the same happening for spoken languages, especially the big, powerful ones.

The sad truth is that interpreting exists in a hierarchy. The amount of prestige it gets seems to be tied to the prestige of your clients. This means that conference interpreting tends to be seen as the most prestigious part of the profession, followed by court interpreting, with public-service interpreting and sign-language interpreting struggling for recognition at the bottom[2].

It takes very little effort to see this hierarchy, as unfair and problematic as it is, as a reason why conference-interpreting associations can negotiate on an almost equal footing with large international organisations and get what they ask for, while representatives of public-service interpreters and sign-language interpreters are ignored when they protest even the most obviously unjust conditions. A simple comparison of the rates of pay for staff interpreters at the EU with those of court interpreters in England and Wales makes it clear.

It doesn't help that interpreters of different types have only recently discovered that they are all equally valid members of the same large, noisy family. Conference interpreting, after all, was professionalised in the 1950s, amidst the birth and growth of the largest and most respected international organisations we recognise today.

The prestige of conference interpreting and its place as the first form of interpreting to be professionalised in the modern era[3] meant that, when the time came for other forms of interpreting to be professionalised, they would turn to the ethical codes established for conference interpreting as models of best practice. We would all start off thinking that neutrality, terminological precision, and striving to be invisible were the pillars of our profession, simply because those were the ethics developed by conference interpreters. Even interpreters themselves fell into this hierarchical thinking.

The spell of conference interpreting and its history and ethics would not even begin to be broken until the 1980s. From that point on, researchers and some interpreters began to question how sustainable such standards actually were in cases where there were pronounced differences between interpreting users in terms of power. Multiple studies were done that also started to question whether those standards represented accurately the type of work interpreters actually did[4]. My personal favourite is the article on medical interpreting by Andrew Clifford, where he argues that sometimes it can be ethical to be slightly inaccurate if it will help people receive the treatment they need[5]. Saving lives trumps perfect technique, it seems.

The growing acceptance that the classical ethics of conference interpreting did not really apply to other forms of interpreting threatened to further divide the profession. Here we had medical interpreters viewing their work one way, court interpreters seeing themselves another way, and conference interpreters sticking to their traditional positions. This is, more or less, the conclusion of Claudia Angelelli's landmark book on how different kinds of interpreters view their work[6].

There was and still is hope, however. In the same year that Andrew Clifford was challenging our views of accuracy and Claudia Angelelli was discovering just how different we thought we were from each other, Ebru Diriker wrote a book that showed that conference interpreters were not immune to adjusting their output, distancing themselves from what some speakers said by changing their pronoun use or even adding their own commentary[7]. It would only be a few years before Morven Beaton (now Beaton-Thome) would point out that even interpreters in the EU itself were not nearly as neutral as we had all thought[8].

If we have proven that no interpreter is ever truly neutral, all this could show that we interpreters, no matter our specialty, face many of the same challenges.

This could provide the basis for unity, but it is not enough in itself to break down the barriers. Injustice, though, is.

We know that there is no good reason to view interpreting at murder trials as less important than conference interpreting for a meeting generated purely by the mores of Euro-bureaucracy. Few interpreters would argue that interpreting for Deaf students is any less cognitively demanding than interpreting at a factory tour or at a negotiation. Yet the only people who are able to argue aggressively and convincingly for the elimination of this unfair hierarchy are interpreters. We are the people who know our work best. The only people with experience in negotiating for the cause of interpreting are the people who have already done it.

Granted, some of us might feel pretty secure at the top of the pile, for the moment at least, but it doesn't take a Nostradamus to see that the future might not necessarily be as bright. The same market forces and political motivations that have threatened court interpreting are beginning to affect conference interpreting, too. The rise of the New Right in Europe is not just about a dislike of Euro-bureaucracy, but a fear of foreignness. It would only take a single politician from the wrong party to argue that all EU staff should speak English for the most secure of conference interpreters to feel at risk.

We need each other. Some interpreters work with groups who are becoming accustomed to lobbying for their rights – rights that include interpreting. Other interpreters have learned how to master social media to spread the truth about our profession far beyond our current circles. And there are some, admittedly few, interpreters who have the ear of senior figures in government and industry. All these connections and all this experience is valuable and must be made to count.

If the greatest challenges of interpreting are to add value and prove that we are adding value, then it will take unity to meet these challenges. In terms of adding value, conference interpreters still tend to stick their traditional ethics. They have lessons to learn from the experiences of business-negotiation interpreters, public-service interpreters, and sign-language interpreters on what it means to work professionally by providing real and tangible added value.

When it comes to appearing to add value, there is something to be said for the success of conference interpreting in convincing clients of its own importance. There is also a lot to be learned from the new band of interpreters who are proudly using Twitter, LinkedIn, Facebook, and face-to-face networking as tools to promote their work. Some clients are listening. More need to be reached.

It is only by pooling our resources and expertise and by attempting to pool our collective prestige and respect that we can make an impact on societies that are becoming increasingly xenophobic and introverted, as well as benefit from those that are becoming increasingly open. We need each other. Interpreters, assemble!

One of the most fruitful ways to increase the unity in our profession is to actually work in more than one setting. It's hard to see your work the same way when you work in conference interpreting, in courts, and in community settings. Some interpreters even combine interpreting with others kinds of language-based work, too. Two of the finest examples of this are Judy and Dagmar Jenner, co-authors of

The Entrepreneurial Linguist, one of the best books available on the business side of translation. Not only are they writers but they work in conference interpreting, court interpreting, and community interpreting, and even offer translation and copywriting. The interview with them covers how they got to that point and how they feel we can improve the unity of our profession.

Interview with Judy and Dagmar Jenner

Between the two of you, you cover conference interpreting, court interpreting, community interpreting, translation, and copywriting. Could you describe how you came to offer this wide range of services?

Great question! We started out as translators and added interpreting (including all the necessary certifications) later because we were really intrigued by interpreting. It turns out that we are quite good at it, and we love the variety of our work. We would probably not love our jobs as much as we do if it weren't for the variety. As translators, we are, of course, first and foremost writers, so we also really enjoy doing copywriting. Once in a while, it all comes together when we write copy for a client that we translate (with our team). While we love community interpreting, it's unfortunately the least recognized and least well-paid of all our services, so we don't do it as often as we'd like. We are huge proponents of doing *pro bono* work, but prefer to work *pro bono* at the association level rather than donating our actual interpreting services. Our hope is to, at some point, make clients see that interpreting services have value, and we think that providing them *pro bono* services might be adverse to that goal. For instance, conference organizers know they cannot get the A/V equipment needed for interpreting for free, simply because companies don't donate their expensive equipment. Yet interpreters are oftentimes expected to donate their time, which doesn't make sense. We need to work together to change that.

Do you notice any difference in how clients approach you when working in different settings?

In conference interpreting settings, we oftentimes have little contact with the end client, but sometimes one will stop by the booth and give us a thumbs-up. Occasionally someone will tell us that it's 'magic', but most of the time, we are part of the professional staff that works in the background, in a way. Judy is a court interpreter, and clients' perceptions vary in the US. Oftentimes, judges seem – to our great dismay – quite bothered to see a certified court interpreter in the courtroom because it slows down the proceedings. However, language access is the law, which doesn't always mean we get treated nicely. For legal cases that are handled outside of court (depositions, arbitration, mediation, etc.), clients, mostly law firms, have to retain the interpreter, and they usually seem very pleased to have us. In community and medical settings, all parties are usually delighted to have us because there's usually a significant language barrier that we have been summoned to bridge.

Together, you wrote the book The Entrepreneurial Linguist. *How do you think interpreters could become more entrepreneurial, especially those who work in court or community settings?*

While we think that we've come a long way, I think we have a long way to go. Especially in the US, court interpreters have been so used to the courts and other entities imposing their rates on them that they stop seeing themselves as having the ability to demand certain rates and get them. However, it goes both ways: to get professional rates, you have to behave like a professional and run a professional business, and you can't do that with a Hotmail email address, a free business card from Vistaprint, and no website. We have to professionalise the profession before we can all get the rates that those at the top command and deserve. We oftentimes ask fellow interpreters: would you hire an attorney whose email address is yourattorney@hotmail.com? The answer is usually: no way! And the same holds true for our profession. We think having a professional email address, website, etc. will be the minimum standard. And then there's customer service: you will get high rates only if you are able to do the job and keep the clients happy. It's not hard to do, yet it's amazing to hear that we are usually the only interpreters who send little gifts to our clients throughout the year and for special occasions. Without clients, you have nothing, so it's essential to keep them happy.

The main thesis of this chapter is that interpreters need to work to close the gap in status between different forms of interpreting. Do you attempt to do this in your own practice? If so, how?

Especially in the United States, Judy has worked on this issue quite extensively, mainly in Nevada, where she resides (specifically, Las Vegas). As the former president of the Nevada Interpreters and Translators Association, Judy has lobbied at the state level for higher rates for court interpreters, and has stopped working at the courts when the rate was lowered drastically. Unfortunately, all the lobbying and refusing to work is only effective when we, as interpreters, work together. That has not always been the case, which is why we appreciate this book about unity and value. In the case of Nevada, most court interpreters accepted the new rate, so nothing changed. However, through outreach and talking with colleagues, judges, legislators, and other people of influence, we've had some success in Nevada. The best way we know of elevating a profession, or of elevating court (and community and medical) interpreting to the heights of conference interpreting, is to refuse work at a level that's too low. But again, that takes critical mass, and we are not there yet. If we could wish for one thing, it would be for more solidarity, for all interpreters to realize that no interpreter is an island – that we are all in this together. You know why some courts and some agencies continue to offer offensively low rates? Because interpreters, even some highly qualified ones, are willing to work for those rates, thus adversely affecting the market for everyone else. We need to start believing that we are worth every penny, because we are.

On the European side, Dagmar has worked tirelessly with the local interpreters and translators association UNIVERSITAS Austria (as a board member and as the Secretary General until March 2015) to promote solidarity and a healthy sense of self-value, especially among the new generation of translators and interpreters. There are workshops for budding interpreters and translators, as well as a mentoring program to assist this process. We have hope that the new generation of interpreters and translators will resist the urge to undersell each other, and that it will proudly charge adequate prices for the work they do. We strongly believe that we are much stronger if we work together instead of against each other. And yes, the pie is big enough for all of us even if we charge adequate prices.

Finally, we both teach interpreting at the college level (Dagmar at the University of Vienna, and Judy at the University of California San Diego–Extension's online program), and we instil in all our students a sense of pride. We try to teach them something that many T&I programs don't teach: business skills and asking for what you want.

How do you think interpreters who only work in one setting could do this?

The best way to increase working conditions and rates, regardless of the field, is to work only for the rate that you think is fair and represents a professional rate, and to set minimum standards and stick to them. The more expensive something is, the more valuable it is usually perceived to be. You'd be surprised how many clients hire us because they want to work with the best – and they don't know anything about our actual skills, but our rates makes them perceive our skills as superb, which is great on all levels.

Traditionally, interpreters in different settings train separately, have separate CPD, and even separate professional associations. What concrete steps do you think professional associations could take to build unity in the profession?

This is an interesting point and it's very true that we've been quite fragmented in the past. This has to do mainly with the fact, we think, that different settings have developed at difference paces, and unfortunately that has created some sort of us-against-them mentality and perhaps an unintended pecking order (AIIC at the top, everyone else at the bottom). That said, we know many interpreters who work in a variety of settings and belong to several associations. We don't know if it's possible to combine some these associations, as some of them go back decades, but we should definitely work on not playing one against the other. In the US, InterpretAmerica has done a great job at providing a forum for all interpreters.

In Austria, while there exist as many as four different associations for interpreters and translators (court interpreting, sign-language interpreting, AIIC, UNIVERSITAS Austria), the latter has evolved into the unofficial 'umbrella' association. There are solid ties between most of these associations.

What sorts of training do you feel would be relevant to all interpreters?

The answer to this question varies greatly on the country and the available training resources, but let's focus on Europe and the US. We think that for court interpreting, some certification is crucial, but of course that's very tough in reality, as there just isn't a full certification for, say, Afrikaans in any country that we know of (outside South Africa, probably). Ideally, all interpreters should have some sort of higher-level training, but much of this is only available in a handful of languages, so we have a long way to go with this. However, most interpreters, regardless of their settings, who take their jobs seriously, acquire education and new skills whenever possible, and we continue to do so as well. Beyond language-specific and interpreting-specific training, interpreters need some business skills, as has already been mentioned in this book. In addition, all interpreters need to believe in their worth – and that's hard to teach. If an individual interpreter does not believe that she or he is worth a certain rate, it's almost impossible to make a client believe it. Last but not least, we are huge believers in collective wisdom. We can learn so much from each other, yet oftentimes we look to outside experts rather than each other. We have grown the most as interpreters when we've attended trainings by our peers who have generously shared what they know, and we do the same thing on our end. We are all stronger together, and interpreters are the only ones who can truly elevate this profession – because we have a vested interest in it.

Key chapter concepts

- The sad truth is that interpreting exists in a hierarchy.
- The only people with experience in negotiating for the cause of interpreting are the people who have already done it.
- We need each other.
- Some clients are listening. More need to be reached.
- All interpreters need to believe in their worth.

Putting it into practice

Let's look at how to take the arguments from the chapter and turn them into work. Given the topic of this chapter, most of the suggestions will be for things we can do as groups. That doesn't mean, however, that we can sit around waiting for others to pick up the slack. On the contrary, it puts the onus on each of us to search for colleagues with whom we can make a difference.

Questions to ask

Where do you think your work sits on the hierarchy? Are you happy with that place?

Who do you think would benefit most from the destruction of the gap in prestige between interpreters in different settings? Does anyone stand to lose?

To what extent do you think the standards and ethics that you were taught are relevant for the type of interpreting you do?

Actions to take

On your own

Subscribe to some blogs written by interpreters working in a different setting than you. Reflect on how similar or different their experiences are from yours. After a few weeks, drop them a supportive email or comment.

Being very honest, take a look at your rates and working practices. Consider what message they are sending to clients and to other interpreters. What effect do you think it would have if you increased your rates by 20 per cent overnight?

Get in contact with a professional association covering a different form of interpreting. See if there is some kind of 'friends' or 'supporter' membership category that would allow you to keep in touch with them.

The next time there is a public or political discussion of interpreting in your home country, contribute to the debate in a way that honours and helps your fellow professionals.

In a group

Unity is best built by groups of interpreters. Lobby your professional association to build bridges with other associations that serve other parts of the profession.

Organise an informal meet-up for interpreters of any kind who live in your area. Use it to build and create friendships across the traditional divides.

Notes

1 You can find my take on that here: http://bit.ly/FakeInterpreter (URL is case sensitive).
2 Daniel Gile, 'Translation Research versus Interpreting Research: Kinship, Differences and Prospects for Partnership', in *Translation Research and Interpreting Research: Traditions, Gaps and Synergies*, edited by Christina Schäffner, 2004, 10–34; J. Cambridge, 'Public Service Interpreting: Practice and Scope for Research', in *Translation Research and Interpreting Research. Traditions, Gaps and Synergies*, edited by C. Schäffner, 2004, 49–51.

3 Some historians would argue that business negotiation and diplomatic interpreting were professionalised much earlier, in Ancient Egypt. See Alfred Hermann, 'Interpreting in Antiquity', in *The Interpreting Studies Reader*, ed. Franz Pöchhacker and Miriam Shlesinger, trans. Ruth Morris (London: Routledge, 1956), 15–22.

4 A list of these can be found in the "Additional Reading" section on the companion website.

5 Andrew Clifford, 'Is Fidelity Ethical?: The Social Role of the Healthcare Interpreter', *TTR: Traduction, Terminologie, Rédaction, 17*, no. 2 (2004). Retrieved from www.erudit.org/revue/ttr/2004/v17/n2/013273ar.html.

6 C. V. Angelelli, *Revisiting the Interpreter's Role: A Study of Conference, Court, and Medical Interpreters in Canada, Mexico, and the United States*, vol. 55 (Amsterdam: John Benjamins Publishing Company, 2004).

7 E. Diriker, *De-/Re-Contextualizing Conference Interpreting: Interpreters in the Ivory Tower?*, vol. 53 (Amsterdam: John Benjamins Publishing Company, 2004).

8 Morven Beaton, 'Interpreted Ideologies in Institutional Discourse: The Case of the European Parliament', *The Translator, 13*, no. 2 (2007): 271–96; Morven Beaton-Thome, 'Negotiating Identities in the European Parliament: The Role of Simultaneous Interpreting', in *Text and Context: Essays on Translation and Interpreting in Honour of Ian Mason*. Manchester: St. Jerome, 2010, 117–38.

Chapter 7

Melting the ivory tower
Keeping research relevant

Chapter summary

This chapter covers:

- Why researchers need help from professionals,
- The kind of research interpreting really needs,
- The benefits of working with researchers.

It's early morning when I leave my sleeping wife and children to head out for a flight to Belfast. That afternoon, I stand in front of students and staff, and argue vehemently that research can and should be tightly connected to the interests and needs of professionals. A few months later, I get up at a similarly unfriendly hour to give much the same message to students and staff in Banská Bystrica, Slovakia: Make research relevant. Work with professionals. Break down the walls. Make a difference.

I have been repeating those phrases since I first discovered exactly how rare it was for research to make any kind of impact outside the arena of academia. But this book is not aimed at researchers. These pages are aimed squarely at practicing interpreters – people who are more likely to be found in conference halls, courts, and doctors' surgeries than lecture halls and libraries. Why should they be bothered about research at all, and, more to the point, how can they even begin to ensure research stays relevant?

If research into interpreting is going to reflect real life in any way, researchers need to work with interpreting professionals. It could be as little as researchers asking interpreters to accompany them into the lab for an experiment or as much as researchers shadowing interpreters for months on end. Whether you think so or not, research and researchers need you.

If research needs you, that gives you power. There are frustratingly few interpreters who are willing to be researched. Fear of mistakes being shown in print, disinterest, and sheer lack of time all contribute. While being researched is slightly scary, it could also be very rewarding. All interpreters want to improve. And, as I mentioned in Chapter 3, we all could do with an extra pair of ears and eyes to monitor our work and give us feedback. Even if all you get out of it is the chance to have someone listen closely to your work, taking part in research offers very real learning opportunities.

These opportunities can only be realised, however, if we ask for them. If researchers are analysing some linguistic or social issue, it makes sense to ask to review their analysis of our work. Better yet, we can offer to give them our take on it. I know very few researchers who would say 'no' to first-hand data like that!

The sad fact is that, for many researchers, doing any kind of useful work on interpreting can be a real problem. Yet without such research, interpreting can't develop. Imagine doctors blocking medical research or lawyers making it difficult for people to do detailed legal studies. It makes no sense at all. It's the same for interpreting. For our professions to grow and for our skills to develop, we need researchers dedicated to advancing what we know and how we can use that knowledge.

I could stop there but there is actually something much bigger going on. For one thing, I deliberately haven't defined what kind of research is useful. Until relatively recently, I would have argued strongly that the most useful research is work that will make interpreters better, give us a louder voice, help us argue for higher fees, and so on. Now, however, I have realised that those things, as important as they are, can only ever be the start.

A simple example can be found in research on clients' expectations of interpreters. While it is pretty common for people to argue that the more we know about clients' expectations, the stronger we will be in negotiations[1], this only goes part of the way. A much more important use of such data would be to adjust how we interpret according to the needs of each client, so we can make sure we are delivering what clients need. If we know the purpose of an event and what our clients want to get out of it, we can help them get that. In other words, the more we know, the more value we can add.

Much the same logic applies to research on the use of untrained interpreters where professionals might be expected. Rather than using such work to rail against injustices, we can look carefully to see if we can uncover patterns. Is it always about money or is it, as I argued in Chapter 1, more to do with the kind of interpreting we are delivering? Are there times when someone who has not been trained as an interpreter can deliver better work than someone who has been trained? If so, what can we learn to do better?

We might think that we know the answers to those kinds of questions, but only research can tell us for sure. Similarly, only research can tell us what it actually means to grow and develop as an interpreter and why some interpreters seem to be unable to do so. Again, we need to be more interested in locating patterns and learning what works than building up cases for what we think we already know.

Where research can really add value to the profession is when it helps us add value to our clients. Remember: the biggest challenges for interpreting are adding value to clients and demonstrating the value we add. It is going to take unprecedented partnership between academia and the profession if we are going to achieve either of those in any meaningful way.

So what does this kind of partnership look like? Let me give you a few examples.

Professor Graham Turner, a researcher in sign language and sign-language interpreting at Heriot-Watt University, has been working with interpreters and Deaf organisations to create research that is helpful for all stakeholders. This has meant working with interpreter-researchers on studying interpreting in such varied contexts as the theatre, courts, and everyday workplaces. The central principle of all of this, in Graham's own words, is that research should be "on, for, and with"[2] those involved in interpreting.

There's also the work of Robyn Dean. Her research has dealt with the complicated issue of interpreter ethics. Rather than stay at the traditional level of 'dos' and 'don'ts', Robyn has worked as an interpreter trainer, researcher, and interpreter to create a much more useful perspective. Working with psychiatry professor Robert Pollard and learning from medical doctors, she has come to the view that interpreters are there to advance the 'goal of the situation' in which they work[3]. If one works in a doctor's surgery, that means helping the patient to be effectively treated. If one works in court, that means helping justice be carried out. If one works in an educational setting, that means helping students learn.

This idea reflects what was stated in the Introduction and is the core argument of this book. One of the most fascinating things that happens when researchers and practitioners work together is that we understand even better what interpreting is really about. We move from seeing interpreting as a linguistic process that happens to involve people to seeing it as a people process involving language.

The truth is that when researchers and practitioners work together, both benefit and both are changed. For practitioners, research gives us enough distance from our everyday concerns to realise that our work is more complex and more powerful than we thought. We can use research to think more critically about anything related to our practice, from how we deal with cognitive overload to how we present ourselves to clients, which leads ultimately to better interpreting. Any part of our work, from preparation and marketing to decision making and follow-up, can and should be the subject of hands-on research.

In a now famous study, Susan Berk-Seligson pointed out that something as small as the frequency of honourifics (e.g. sir, ma'am, your honour) can affect how people perceive the witness. If a witness or defendant uses them too much, he or she can be seen as uneducated and untrustworthy, yet if used too little, he or she may seem rude[4]. The starkest part of this study is that court interpreters are normally told simply to repeat what the witness said, yet by doing so, it seems that they could be contributing to injustice by giving the jury a possibly misleading impression. Here again is a place where interpreters can add value by taking the time to give culturally relevant versions, whenever we are given the chance.

On slightly more familiar and less controversial terrain, Martin Djovčoš and his wife Zuzana Djovčošova have investigated how to help interpreters improve their language processing – increasing the value we add by helping us to work more efficiently. Their research has suggested that exercises used to treat patients that have aphasia – a range of disorders affecting language comprehension and production – can be useful for interpreters, too. Simple exercises such as repeating sentences but omitting redundant information or answering questions quickly in a different language to the one in which they were posed[5] can help us train our brain to function more effectively.

Lastly, research offers some useful initial perspective for those of us involved in telephone interpreting. Here, Uldis Ozolins has surveyed the available research and has suggested that the well-known constraints of this mode of interpreting should lead to us to reconsider our established practices. Switching over to using third-person pronouns ('he said'/'she said') might prove to be necessary to facilitate understanding and useful turn-taking patterns, especially with those interpreters who are new users of this mode[6]. In short, the lack of visual cues in telephone interpreting means that interpreters simply must take on the role of managing the entire encounter[7]. Lessons learned in such an established form of remote interpreting could prove vital if we are to use the newer forms that are appearing, which benefit from the recent growth in broadband access and speeds to offer us visual information, too.

Interpreters need research so we can grow and develop. Research needs interpreters so it can be grounded in real life. The real question is 'how can we work together effectively?' That is one of the subjects that will be covered in the interview with Professor Ebru Diriker, whose book, *De-/Re-Contextualizing Conference Interpreting: Interpreters in the Ivory Tower?*, looked at how people view conference interpreting in Turkey and whether the work performed by actual interpreters at a philosophy conference conformed to that image.

Interview with Ebru Diriker

Your book, De-/Re-Contextualizing Conference Interpreting: Interpreters in the Ivory Tower?, *is known for comparing the way that interpreters often talk about their work with the way they actually performed at one particular conference. Could you briefly summarise the background to the book and what you discovered?*

During the 1990s, when I started my PhD on interpreting studies, translation studies had already taken the 'cultural turn', and there were lots of conceptual and empirical research on interdependency between the translator, their working processes, the actual translations they produced, and their social context. Concepts such as neutrality, impartiality, and what constitutes ethical practice were all being critically reviewed. Community-interpreting research, which also sharply focused on the contextual and human factors in interpreting, had started to gain visibility. My own area of interest, conference interpreting, on the other hand, had set up its base camp in cognitive and psycholinguistic approaches. It had also witnessed the development of the 'theory of sense' by Danica Seleskovitch, which argued that the main task of interpreters was to transfer the *meanings* intended by the speakers and not their words. This theory had freed the field from a strictly linguistic straitjacket in the 1970s and opened up horizons, but it had also been adopted somewhat superficially by the profession, and to some extent academia, so that conference-interpreting research still had not started investigating how interpreters influence and are influenced by the interpreting setting in which they thrive as professionals.

The readings I made for the PhD courses at Boğaziçi University, especially Cecilia Wadensjö's book, *Interpreting as Interaction,* and Franz Pöchhacker's *Simultandolmetschen als Komplexes Handeln,* greatly influenced my thinking. These books, coupled with my own experience as a conference interpreter, increased my awareness of the gap between the way the outside world sees interpreting and what interpreters do in real-life situations. I therefore decided to compare and contrast the representation and professional image of conference interpreters with actual interpreting performance.

I first tried to understand the professional image of conference interpreting by looking at what people say about interpreting in dictionaries, encyclopaedias, popular books, the media, academia, and interpreters' own discourse. The results were quite interesting. Both insiders and outsiders were keen on emphasising 'fidelity to the original' as a key aspect of interpreting. The difference was that outsiders to the profession emphasised that interpreters remained faithful to the *words* uttered by the speaker, whereas insiders, i.e. the interpreters, emphasised that interpreters remained faithful to the *meaning* intended by the speaker. Interestingly, while emphasising that their task was to remain faithful to the original meaning, interpreters also referred to striking instances where they became actively involved in the interpretation process when they were asked to recount real-life instances and hence, 'contextualise' interpreting.

My next step was to try to compare and contrast this image with real-life interpreting behaviour. I was hoping to record a political conference, but received permission to record a conference organised by the Philosophy Department of my university on 'Heidegger and Arendt: Metaphysics and Politics'. Initially, the topic seemed very abstract and far from what I had hoped for, but the results turned out to be quite revealing. In contrast to the idealised professional image of conference interpreters, the performance of the interpreter in real-life contexts was not only limited to 'reproducing the meaning intended by the speaker', but involved active participation in negotiating the meaning and co-constructing the interaction. Interpreters not only conveyed the speaker's utterances but also regulated turn-taking, resolved overlapping speech, addressed their listeners directly, blended explanatory or compensatory remarks into the speaker's words, and even voiced their comments and criticisms against the speaker. These results point to a more complex co-presence of the interpreter in the interpretation process and product than we tend to think.

*In early 2015, you did a guest lecture at Manchester University on clients' expec-
tations of conference interpreting. Why do you think this work has failed to capture
the attention of practising interpreters?*

I believe that research results do impress practicing interpreters once they hear
about them. I have had the chance to present research results in institutions such as
the European Parliament, one of the largest employers of conference interpreters,
and seen how interested people become when they realise this academic field has
something relevant to say about their daily practice.

Like with many other professions, I think there is an overall lack of communication between researchers and professionals. Professionals are busy people and
rightfully believe they have already acquired the necessary skills and knowledge
to practice the profession. They tend to think academia deals more with theoret-
ical and abstract issues, and do not always show an eagerness to read research.
Academics, on the other hand, do not always do a good job of presenting research
results in a way that will appeal to the first-hand experiences of a practicing professional, either. There are also few contact points where research can meet the practitioner. I believe the International Association of Conference Interpreters (AIIC)
does a good job of presenting research results to its members, but could do even
better. Local associations could become more active and universities should definitely become more active in reaching out to the professionals, inviting them to
public lectures and seminars with the understanding that research results must be
presented differently from the typical academic format. I have seen some valuable
efforts go down the drain when brilliant researchers fail to make a connection between their research and the reality of the practitioner. In interpreting studies, most
researchers are practicing interpreters themselves, so I believe, with some effort,
establishing this connection should be easier for most of us.

*As well as being a researcher, you are also a practising conference interpreter.
How has your interpreting work affected your research?*

I believe it has had a profound impact on the way I read, interpret, and do research.
Being both an insider and an outsider has considerable advantages, because you
can detect 'interesting' points in your daily practice and later on delve more closely into these issues. Being an insider and outsider at the same time also allows
one to scan whether a research question makes sense from both research and interpreting points of view. This comes in very handy when one reviews others'
research and supervises young researchers from both inside and outside the field
of interpreting. However, there is also a flip side. For the same reasons, one also
needs to approach one's own biases as critically as possible. Being an insider and
outsider is difficult and one might easily have blind spots of which one is unaware.
I mentioned my own thesis-writing process, where I was very keen on recording a
political conference, because I knew most political conferences created a number
of challenges for the interpreters. But then circumstances forced me to focus on a

conference on philosophy and many interesting points emerged rather unexpectedly at a place where I would expect to find very little. Given that there is no remedy to overcome one's bias, one should at least be aware that they exist and colour the way we see things.

Interpreters commonly argue that interpreting research relates only very tenuously to practice. How would you respond to this view?

I actually find most research on interpreting highly relevant for the profession and the professionals. For instance, it is very interesting to learn that the way we wear our headsets is related to our ear preference or to understand that to overcome a mediocre performance we need continuous 'deliberate practice'. I believe the way we present the results and our failure to link findings with the realities of the practitioners play a role in this perception. We cannot expect all professionals to read and enjoy academic journals. We also cannot expect them to enjoy academic discourse. We must work on how we can 'popularise' research, and I also believe we must take the first step in reaching out to the professionals. Some of them might resist the idea no matter what we do and how relevant we make our research, but I am sure many will gradually develop a closer interest to the field.

I know from my own experience that graduates of interpreting schools who have taken courses in interpreting theory and research at university are much more inclined to follow research and stay connected with academia. Since the number of interpreters who graduate from university programs is on the rise, we should pay close attention to the design and delivery of such courses at the university level.

In the chapter, I give a few example of researchers and practitioners working together to carry out research that will be useful to both. What is your favourite example of this kind of teamwork?

I could cite many examples of fascinating research carried out by researchers in studies of interpreting who are practitioners and who worked in collaboration with researchers from other disciplines. Franco Fabbro and Laura Gran's cooperation in the 1990s at Trieste University, for instance, paved the way to neurolinguistics research on interpreting. Other personal favourites include Miriam Shlesinger and Morton Ann Gernsbacher's cooperation on the cognitive mechanism of suppression and Barbara Moser-Mercer's recent cooperation with neuroscientists at Geneva University on the neural correlates of simultaneous interpreting. All of these interdisciplinary efforts have given very fruitful results.

Lastly, if you could give one piece of advice to interpreters who want to work fruitfully with researchers, what would it be?

Do try to help out as much as you can. Most interpreting research will pay back its debt by expanding the horizons in this field!

Key chapter concepts

- Break down the walls. Make a difference.
- If research needs you, that gives you power.
- The more we know, the more value we can add.
- We need to be more interested in locating patterns and learning what works than building up cases for what we think we already know.
- Most interpreting research will pay back its debt by expanding the horizons in this field.

Putting it into practice

Questions to ask

What is your current attitude to research? How did that come about? What would it take to change it?

If researchers could discover one thing about interpreting, what do you think it should be?

Actions to take

On your own

Contact your nearest interpreting university and ask them if they need anyone for experimental or qualitative work. Offer them your services.

For the next month, pick one area of your professional practice and try to find one or two papers to read on it. After you have read them, send a polite email to the authors with your thoughts.

In a group

Work with a few other interpreters on a joint research project on your experiences. It could be on different negotiation approaches, new technological tools or anything else. Start with something informal to help you all understand what it is like to think deeply about your own practice together.

Professional associations could attempt to build closer links with universities, asking for research on the topics that most interest them and contributing to relevant academic conferences.

Notes

1 For example, I. Kurz, 'Conference Interpreting: Quality in the Ears of the User', *Meta*, *46*, no. 2 (2001): 394–409; G. Mack and L. Cattaruzza, 'User Surveys in SI: A Means of Learning about Quality and/or Raising Some Reasonable Doubts', in *Topics in Interpreting Research*, ed. Jorma Tommola (Turku: University of Turku, Centre for Translation and Interpreting, 1995), 37–51.
2 Graham H. Turner and Frank Harrington, 'Issues of Power and Method in Interpreting Research', in *Intercultural Faultlines: Research Models in Translation Studies*, ed. Maeve Olohan, Research Models in Translation Studies 1 (Manchester: St Jerome Publishing, 2000), 253–65.
3 Robyn K. Dean and Robert Q. Pollard Jr, 'Beyond "Interesting": Using Demand Control Schema to Structure Experiential Learning', in *In Our Hands: Educating Healthcare Interpreters*, ed. K. Malcolm and L. Swabey (Washington, DC.: Gallaudet University Press, 2012), 77–104.
4 Susan Berk-Seligson, *The Bilingual Courtroom: Court Interpreters in the Judicial Process* (Chicago: University of Chicago Press, 2002).
5 Martin Djovčoš and Zuzana Djovčošova, 'Aphasia and Interpreting: Aphasia-Based Interpreting Exercises', *FORUM*, *11*, no. 1 (2013): 42–44.
6 Uldis Ozolins, 'Telephone Interpreting: Understanding Practice and Identifying Research Needs', *Translation & Interpreting*, *3*, no. 2 (27 February 2012): 38–39. doi: 10.12807/t&i.v3i2.136.
7 *Ibid.*, 40.

Chapter 8

Boosting your brain and body

Eating your way to success

Chapter summary

This chapter covers:

- Why physical fitness is more important than we think,
- Some surprising candidates for good interpreter food,
- How to start the process of good health for long-term results.

It wasn't until the second visit to the physio that I realised something was up. I would wake up one day with legs that felt relatively fine and the next with the feeling that someone had replaced my knees with small lumps of wet cabbage. To make it worse, on a 'bad knee day', walking, turning, and bending sent me reaching for painkilling cream.

At the first appointment, the physio asked me about me some simple questions. When he asked me if I did any exercise, I asked if sprinting to the shared printer counted. When he asked about stretches, I told him I stretched my mind. When he asked about the physical demands of the job, I asked if fitting into small booths counted.

"There you have it," he said, in a very medical fashion. "Your problem is your job."

That didn't mean much to me until the next session, when he localised the problem.

The diagnosis? It wasn't my knees that were dodgy, but the muscles around them. The only way to solve the problem was to start a course of leg exercises which, to this day, provide great entertainment to my wife and children.

Interpreters aren't normally associated with fitness. No teenager pins up pictures of SCIC staff (Directorate-General for Interpretation of the European Commission) on their bedroom walls. Your local court interpreter is not likely to be signing a deal with *Vogue* any time soon. To put it scientifically, we have 'sedentary occupations'. We sit, we talk, we look for food. We sit and talk and go home.

Of course, no one hires us for our ability to beat Usain Bolt in a race or to carry weights. Well, maybe they should. We might work every day with our brains, mouths, hands, ears, and eyes, but what powers all of that is our bodies. Our bodies are powered by our diet and exercise regimes. Fitness is about far more than just managing to walk up the stairs to a medical interpreting assignment without becoming short of breath.

Successful interpreters want to keep getting better. Few people would argue that getting better means doing something to improve how our brains perform on the job. All the note-taking classes in the world won't help if your memory is like a broken sieve and your problem-solving skills stop at opening chocolate bar wrappers.

With that in mind, two scientific studies should be on your reading list for your next journey. Stanley Colcombe and Arthur Kramer[1] and a team led by Yu-Kai Chang[2] both set out to examine whether regular exercise routines could help people perform better at mental tasks. The result in both studies was that, while exercise does have a small benefit to your performance overall, the biggest improvement was found in tasks where you have to think and coordinate different areas of your brain to work together. One of the tasks they tested was a verbal-fluency task, such as asking people to name lots of animals in a short space of time.

If you have done any interpreting, you will know that those two skills – verbal fluency and controlling different mental processes – cover a large proportion of our work. People have been teaching interpreters about mental efforts for years[3]. As important as it is to have a good memory and a nice voice, the skills of managing everything that is going on when you interpret and of coming up with the right word are vital.

Quite simply, if we want to interpret efficiently and well, those studies show that we need to start going to the gym or running the track regularly. Both of these studies go further, however. To start with, as you age, the benefits of regular exercise increase. In other words, if you are still young enough to wonder how anyone could have ever interpreted before free WiFi, you might get away with delaying your visit to a personal trainer for a little bit. If, on the other hand, you can tell people about interpreting at assignments on the Millennium Bug, it is probably time that you located a pair of shorts and a sweatband.

The second important finding is that jogging to the shops once a week and calling it 'exercise' won't be enough. The best results were found when people undertook exercise sessions of over 20 minutes on a regular basis. What's more, it seems that if we want the effects to last longer, the exercise needs to be more intense[4].

Some people will smile with delight at those findings while others will break into a sweat at the mere thought of trying to find the time to run on a regular basis. The point is not that we should all be aiming to compete in the next Olympics but simply that we need to learn to look after the bodies God has given us. I realise that the schedules of some interpreters would seem low on space and high on stress. And I grant that some interpreters have to deal with rates so low that membership of a private gym and trainer's fees might seem out of reach. However, these are merely hurdles to jump, if you'll pardon the pun.

As with every other area in this book, we need to start where we are. Take my case, for instance. To my relief, my physio said I was not to do any intense exercise (great!), until I can do my leg exercises three times a day without any pain (not so great). That was my starting point. We know that exercising at the gym without proper prep is asking for an injury. Before we go to that level, or invest in an expensive tracksuit and trainers, you need to assess *your* starting point.

There is no excuse for starting and ending each day with a three-hour Netflix binge. If that's your starting point, it is a good reason to book an appointment with a doctor or other health professional to get guidance on what you should and should not be attempting at the beginning. It is also a reason to look for small changes you can make to build your fitness, prepare for the day when you can deal with the amounts and kinds of exercise that will make a difference in the long term.

One small but often overlooked change might be breakfast. I am no dietician – in my home country, people eat deep-fried Mars bars and call it a delicacy – but I can spot a good idea. A team led by David Benton[5] has given me just such an idea. They found that when people ate a healthy breakfast that released glucose slowly into the bloodstream (plain biscuits, wholegrains, and the like), they performed better on mental tasks than people whose breakfast gave them a sugar shot (most breakfast cereals and cereal bars). In other words, changing your sugary breakfast to one with healthful grains and protein, you can help yourself get a head start on healthy living.

What's in your cup is important to look at, too. The humble cup of tea or glass of wine might be of use, as it seems that the compounds in those two drinks, as well as in chocolate and blueberry, help our brains to lay down long-term memories and generally stay healthier[6]. Of course, those four substances need to be taken in moderation. We are not going to do ourselves any favours by downing the entire bottle of wine and following it up with a giant chocolate biscuit dipped in a bowl of sugary tea. In moderation, however, we can eat and drink our way to a healthier brain and body.

The lesson from all of this is simple: look after your kit and it will look after you. We can't afford to take it for granted that our brains and bodies will keep performing at our expected level unless we adopt the practices to maintain them. Little changes add up over time. Change your breakfast, take the stairs, have a cup of tea, nibble some high-cocoa-content chocolate – they sound like easy steps to make, but they are important ones.

In Chapter 3, I discussed creating a CPD plan. Perhaps it's time we all created diet and exercise plans, too. Our collective addictions to caffeine and sugary foods need to be rethought. We need to learn as much about our diets and bodies as we know about the languages we speak.

There is no one better placed to give us the rundown on how to use our diet to improve our performance than Kamil Celoch. A conference interpreter in his own right, Kamil has dedicated his spare time to researching how to enhance our brain power using food and supplements.

Interview with Kamil Celoch

You are most well-known for your ongoing work on interpreter nutrition. Could you tell us how you got started in the subject?

As a former university-level athlete, I have always been interested in improving performance by any and all means at my disposal. What surprised me was that many of the lifestyle and dietary interventions yielded extremely positive changes on what could be widely defined as 'cognition'. It could be argued that 'you are what you eat' is more than just a cliché – according to nutritionist Dr Mark Hyman, even if our genetic makeup plays an important role in how we feel and perform, environmental factors and nutrition are not to be underestimated, as they can switch certain genes on and off, which in turn can have a host of downstream effects on our mood and cognitive performance. This seems to resonate with my experience as an interpreter – I feel and perform at my best when my diet is in check.

One of your most surprising findings was that caffeine, often seen as the interpreter's best friend, might actually be reducing our performance. Could you explain a bit more about this?

Caffeine is certainly an interesting drug. I think it important to note that coffee might have slightly different effects from pure caffeine found in energy drinks and pills, as coffee beans contain some other psychoactive alkaloids as well as antioxidants. Therefore, some people might react better to isolated caffeine as opposed to coffee or even green tea, and likewise, the opposite can also be true for your average java lover.

Sadly, it appears that if you want to rediscover that initial euphoric jolt, you might need to stop caffeine completely for at least a week. This is due to a built-up tolerance, which more coffee will not fix. I am willing to bet my left, now relatively caffeine-free kidney, that I am not the only interpreter who learned this the hard way. Unfortunately, cessation of caffeinated beverages is associated with rather nasty withdrawal symptoms, ranging from lethargy, apathy, and anxiety to reduced cognitive performance, which is why a lot of people prefer to stay in the state of dependence. After all, all you need is just a quick fix of your caffeinated poison of choice and you are ready to rock and roll again, a phenomenon that partly explains the addictive properties of the compound.

Still, caffeine is relatively safe if consumed in moderation, it's easy to obtain and therefore is conducive to support dependence. Many of us also enjoy the taste of coffee. Also, there is a plethora of research that shows that the properties of caffeine are synergistic with an amino acid theanine, especially within the realms of cognitive performance as it pertains to attention and subjective stress levels.

And what would be a better way to replenish our energy levels and concentration capacity during an assignment?

I am afraid that once you get to 'during' stage, your options are rather limited. Sugar-laden snacks and energy drinks might be temporarily effective, but are likely to make you crash shortly after consumption. Small amounts of coconut oil, on the other hand, do not cause spikes in insulin levels but still 'feed' your brain and give you more steady energy levels. Deep breathing is also another great strategy to ensure better performance and reduced stress levels by increasing oxygen levels to the brain. Due to the complexity of bodily processes involved in achieving superior cognitive performance, one has to develop a holistic approach to address all of the following areas:

- *Diet:* reduce inflammation levels, normalise insulin sensitivity, and eliminate food sensitivities and/or allergies; increase intake of micronutrients and omega 3s
- *Hormones:* find and correct any deficiencies; reduce overall stress levels
- *Neurotransmitter balance:* high-protein diet to supply adequate amounts of amino acids; high intake of fruit and vegetables and micronutrients to support healthy enzymatic conversion
- *Mitochondria:* high-intensity interval training (such as sprinting or rowing); limit toxin exposure and inflammation-induced excessive free-radical production
- *Exercise:* ideally at least 20 minutes every day, both anaerobic and aerobic exercise
- *Rest:* meditation; adequate amounts of sleep and naps whenever possible; learn how to unwind without the use of your computer/mobile screen

You have also researched the use of dietary supplements in interpreting. Are there any you would specifically recommend?

Of course, it's hard to make blanket statements, as we all have unique brain chemistries, but I would personally love to see research on tyrosine in an interpreting setting. This naturally occurring amino acid is a precursor to dopamine and its metabolites, and has shown a lot of promise in military research in improving vigilance, stress response, as well as general well-being in sleep-deprived subjects. As you might be aware, one AIIC study has found that burn-out rates in conference interpreters are higher than those of senior-level Israeli army officers. Some anecdotal reports suggest that tyrosine indeed could be an effective tool for a language professional, however at this point we need more research to draw any conclusions. There are also some situation-specific supplements that have been shown to have a high degree of efficacy in the following areas:

- *Fatigue:* rhodiola rosea
- *Focus and attention:* combination of theanine and caffeine, nicotine, tyrosine

- *Chronic stress exposure:* rhodiola rosea, bacopa monnieri
- *Energy production:* a combination of mitochondrial supplements: Alpha-Lipoic Acid, Acetyl-l-Carnitne, Creatine, Resveratrol, Co-Enzyme Q10, Magnesium

Some people seem to thrive on stimulants. Surprisingly, nicotine (not to be confused with cigarettes and tobacco) appears to be a potent cognitive enhancer.

In all your work, you clearly point out that interpreters should run any change in diet past their doctors. Could you give us some examples of how some substances like gluten or caffeine might have different effects on different people?

Caffeine is an interesting example. Some people are slow metabolisers, and, in general, those individuals do not do tolerate the compound all that well. If that wasn't bad enough, it takes longer for the slow metabolisers to clear the caffeine out of their system – a classic double whammy: more side effects for longer! Gluten sensitivity, on the other hand, is more cunning in its ways due to a delayed onset of symptoms. So you eat your favourite croissant on Monday and might not get any symptoms until Wednesday or Thursday! Gluten sensitivity is also harder to pick up in diagnostic tests, since most of them check for full-blown allergies. You might want to consider going gluten free for a week and compare your energy and concentration levels to determine how much, if any, impact this somewhat-hard-to-digest protein has on your well-being.

Do you think interpreters in different settings – such as court interpreters, conference interpreters, or medical interpreters – might have different nutritional needs?

In my view, nutritional needs should be reviewed on an individual basis, irrespective of occupation. Diet and resultant deficiencies are highly variable from person to person, and as such it would be next to impossible to extrapolate with any degree of certainty what nutritional needs an individual might have, let alone a group of professionals. I have a strong suspicion, however, that just like the majority of the population, interpreters would do well to increase their intake of magnesium in their diet, as it is one of the most common deficiencies. Zinc, vitamin D3, and vitamin K2 are also notoriously low in a typical Western diet.

Many interpreters travel a lot for assignments, and some may not have easy access to healthy food options. Could you perhaps suggest some portable snacks that might help them?

Beef jerky, nuts, rice cakes, nut butters, protein powder, fruit, hummus, boiled eggs, seeds, cocktail prawns, and leftovers of last night's dinner are all good options. Remember to include moderate amounts of protein in each and every snack and drink ample amounts of water in between assignments to stay hydrated. Alternatively, you could eat a more substantial, healthy meal every four to five hours if it fits your schedule. In this case you can forego the snacks.

Lastly, if you could suggest one single change that interpreters could make to their diet to improve their performance, what would it be?

Plan your meals ahead to avoid overreliance on sugary snacks – your body and mind will thank you later!

Key chapter concepts

- We might work every day with our brains, mouths, hands, ears and eyes, but what powers all of that is our bodies.
- If we want to interpret efficiently and well, we need to start going to the gym or running the track regularly.
- We need to start where we are.
- Look after your kit and it will look after you.
- I feel and perform at my best when my diet is in check.

Putting it into practice

Questions to ask

How much effort do you put into your physical fitness?

What sorts of food do you eat while preparing for assignments and when you are on them?

Are those foods good or bad for your performance?

When was the last time you had a full medical check-up to spot any areas where you need to improve?

Actions to take

Note: it is always advisable to run any changes past a doctor. The advice in this chapter does not replace close medical supervision and professional training.

On your own

Ask your doctor to book you in for a full check-up to check for any problem areas. Create an action plan for at least one area that needs improvement.

For the next week, so long as you do not have any pre-existing medical condition, consider changing to a breakfast that has a low glycaemic index (GI) and note any changes in your concentration.

Look at the foods that you use for fuel when you are busy or stressed. Change one or two at a time to substances that are more healthful.

In a group

Form a healthy-interpreters group in your local area and train together. The camaraderie and accountability will be a big help in keeping your routine on track.

Notes

1 Stanley Colcombe and Arthur F. Kramer, 'Fitness Effects on the Cognitive Function of Older Adults a Meta-Analytic Study', *Psychological Science, 14*, no. 2 (2003): 125–30.
2 Yu-Kai Chang *et al.*, 'The Effects of Acute Exercise on Cognitive Performance: A Meta-Analysis', *Brain Research*, no. 1453 (2012): 87–101.
3 D. Gile, 'Testing the Effort Models' Tightrope Hypothesis in Simultaneous Interpreting-A Contribution', *Hermes, 23*, no. 1999 (1999): 153–172; Daniel Gile, *Basic Concepts and Models for Interpreter and Translator Training*, vol. 8 (Amsterdam: John Benjamins Publishing Company, 2009).
4 Chang *et al.*, 'The Effects of Acute Exercise on Cognitive Performance', 95.
5 David Benton *et al.*, 'The Delivery Rate of Dietary Carbohydrates Affects Cognitive Performance in Both Rats and Humans', *Psychopharmacology, 166*, no. 1 (2003): 86–90.
6 Jeremy PE Spencer, 'Food for Thought: The Role of Dietary Flavonoids in Enhancing Human Memory, Learning and Neuro-Cognitive Performance', *Proceedings of the Nutrition Society, 67*, no. 02 (2008): 238–52.

Chapter 9

Laughing at ourselves
Seeing the funny side

Chapter summary

This chapter covers:

- Why and how interpreting is funny,
- Humour that helps and humour that hurts,
- The benefits of seeing the funny side of our work.

I was once part of a team of eight interpreters working at an event run by a manufacturer of construction trucks. The first day was tough: simultaneous interpreting in booths with two-inch gaps at the back, as the whole event was taking place in a tent, propped up on ground that I will charitably call 'somewhat uneven'. Eight hours of product and show videos, engineer-speak, soundbites, and walk-arounds later, we open the booth doors and step gingerly out. We were soon greeted by the face of the site manager.

"Erm, you're not going to wear those clothes tomorrow, are you?" he said, a little nervously.

"Why do you ask?" said eight besuited interpreters simultaneously.

"Well, tomorrow, we will be at the test site. It has been raining heavily for three days. It will be one gigantic mud pile. Bring your wellies."

He was right. While some of our colleagues were basking in the glamour of conference halls in Vienna, stadia in Madrid, or hotels in Frankfurt, we were interpreting into hand-held radio microphones, feet squelching in mud, in another tent, waiting for the lunchtime pies to be delivered. To this day, I have no idea how we coped with the glamour.

Interpreting can be funny, if you think about it. What other job can involve wandering through fields while clients try out backhoe loaders, sitting in a doctor's office trying to work out the right way of interpreting the word 'wabbit'[1] into Spanish, or having a long discussion with colleagues on whether Liverpudlian accents would sound good to clients in court?

Of course, interpreting can also be very serious. Some of us have people's lives in our hands. People really live or die, gain or lose their livelihoods, and make or break deals because of interpreters. The rest of this book bears ample testament to the need for us to take our work seriously, take the needs of our clients seriously, and work like the professionals and businesspeople we need to be.

Yet, in all that seriousness, knowing all that we know about the power and purpose and potential of interpreting, we need humour. It is actually because of all those things that we need humour. Interpreting is too serious not to be laughed at and too important to go without jokes.

If that all seems a bit questionable, let me demonstrate something. For sixty seconds, put down this book and pick up a pen. For a minute only, jot down the problems you see in the interpreting world today. These could be anything from low rates of pay to predatory clients to lack of coffee. Go do that now. The book will still be here when you get back (providing your e-reader doesn't crash or you don't inadvertently drop the book).

Done? Good.

You probably have a list of imposing issues that seem absolutely pressing and must be solved. Some of them might seem like real, imminent threats to the future of your career, while others might seem that they are going to make interpreting much less fun than it currently is.

Being realistic now, how many of them do you look at and say, "That looks like great joke material"? Probably very few. Can you think of a side-splitting one-liner about the reduction in court interpreter pay? Do you guffaw at the possibility that we might all be interpreting remotely in ten years' time? (We might leave the house even less than translators!)

I am sure that all of those problems are crying out for a solution. How can we solve the crisis caused by some clients wanting to tighten budgets until our pay consists of half an orange and a second-hand 'thank you' card? How do we solve the issues raised by machine interpreting?

In many cases, we can't directly force people to do something, and, as yet, few of us have enough influence to have politicians pass laws against things we don't like. The future of interpreting is going to require huge doses of creativity. As I said in the Introduction, the problems we face now simply cannot be solved by the systems we inherited from our predecessors. New contexts create new problems. New problems need new solutions.

As odd as it might sound, one key to increasing creativity is humour. According to Josephine Chinying Lang and Chay Hoon Lee[2], in contexts where humour is present, people tend to be more creative. The precise relationship seems to be quite subtle, however. The researchers apparently discovered three functions of humour. One type, liberating humour, simply involves people playing with the rules of culture, logic, and convention. People take ideas from one area and apply them somewhere else. For interpreters, liberating humour might look like this:

> Scientists have discovered that conference interpreters share DNA
> with goldfish: they live in see-through containers, have been known
> to go round in circles for hours, open their mouths repeatedly with no

noise coming out and have ten-second memories. And have ten-second memories.

Silly? Yes it is. It takes ideas from several areas and merges them together for an effect which I hope is comic. Or what about these two?

I try to avoid consecutive interpreting. It scares the Rozan out of me.

You know you married an interpreter when their plans for the evening include a nice dinner, watching a film (and criticising the subtitling) and four hours of terminology research.

Compare this kind of humour to stress-relieving humour. This type of humour does what it says on the tin. It is produced in difficult circumstances as a defence mechanism. You can't change anything, so you muck about a bit and see if you can get a laugh. A good example of this might be a client waiting outside of a court-room and telling anyone who passes that they hope the judges here are nicer than the ones on TV talent shows.

Lastly, there is controlling humour. This is where humour is used as a tool to punish or exclude behaviour that is seen to go against the norm. This kind of humour includes making fun of people, sarcastic comments, parody, and certain kinds of satire. This is humour with a deliberate and calculated sting.

Guess which of these kinds of humour fosters creativity? According to Lang and Lee, it is the first and only the first[3]. It is only when we allow ourselves to think outside of our current circumstances, when we create absurd combinations and illogical paradoxes, that we create space for our brains to do the hard work of coming up with solutions to real problems.

Humour, used well, seems to help us be more creative. How would you react if you were presented with a cork board, a candle, a box of tacks, a book of matches, and a wall, and asked to attach the candle to the wall in such a way that wax would not drip on the floor when it was lit? Granted, it doesn't sound much like a problem a lot of interpreters face, but it was the problem used by Alice Isen of the University of Maryland, Baltimore County, and her team to see whether humour could help people solve problems more effectively[4].

In their experiments, they compared the success rates of people who watched a five-minute funny video with people who received a chocolate bar, people who watched a sad video, people who did five minutes of exercise, and people who just went straight into the task. Whatever the setup, the people who watched the funny video were far more likely to solve the problem than any other group.

But humour can do more than help us solve problems. A team of researchers led by Michelle Tugade found that humour can help people cope better with difficult and stressful situations[5]. And we all know how difficult and stressful interpreting can be sometimes.

But how do we get there? Few of the issues we can list in sixty seconds or sixty minutes seem ripe for witty responses. Those that do might seem to inspire controlling or mocking humour rather than the helpful, liberating kind. Are we doing anyone any favours by spending time thinking about ways to make court interpreting funny? Should we even be going there?

Let's compare humour to the alternative. Probably the most common response to the stresses and strains of working in interpreting is to complain. We write to politicians and newspapers, set up Facebook groups against issues, hold placards, leave sarcastic Twitter messages, share depressing news stories. We are all familiar with this type of response.

Now, as cathartic as it can be to respond this way, what is the end result? Very rarely, if ever, do these actions produce anything that could be classed as 'change' or 'value'. I have yet to see low-paying clients change their ways after interpreters complained. I haven't ever read of a government official saying, "Wow, your stinging rebuke really caught me there. Here, have a 50 per cent rate increase".

All our attempts at criticism, rebuke, and shaming can ever do is get us depressed. Unless we can turn our frustration into action, nothing ever changes. What we need is creativity and positivity, not bemoaning our situation.

As any writer, comedian, or artist will tell you, creativity is not something you can schedule. You can't say, "Today, between 3pm and 5pm, I will be creative". Creativity needs to be encouraged, pursued, and practised. In my own experience, I have found that creativity needs safe spaces where it can bloom – spaces where the end result is less important than the process, and where you are safe from critics, at least to begin with.

One incredibly useful space for creativity is in humour. I learned to write more effectively by putting together slightly cheeky articles for the satirical website Speculative Grammarian[6], and playing around with one-liners on Mr Interpreters' Translation and Interpreting Humour, my Tumblr blog[7]. To this day, I know that if I need a creative solution to a problem, I should start by spending twenty minutes scribbling silly jokes on what it is like to interpret at a nuclear power plant before I even look at the problem. Creativity in humour breeds a creative solution.

So, the short answer is yes, we really do need to go there. We need to look deliberately at our regular work and find humour in it. We need cartoons about interpreters being like secret agents, or hamsters, or goldfish. It really will be helpful to imagine what would happen if interpreters ruled the world (caffeine would be a human right, reading out a talk word-for-word would be an offence, primary-age children would be taught the difference between translators and interpreters, etc.).

We absolutely need space and time to turn our attention from all the reasons why interpreting is hard and toward all the things that make interpreting fun and enjoyable and even hilarious. Here is another exercise: put down the book again, and for sixty seconds, write down all the funniest things that have happened to you or around you while working.

If you did that exercise, you will definitely notice a difference in your mood compared to the last writing exercise. As we stare at the problems, they become bigger and we begin to wonder whether we really want to be doing our job any more. As we look intentionally for the fun and the funny, we suddenly remember why we did that course, why we chose those clients, why we entered this weird and wonderful world in the first place.

One last exercise: pick one part of your business that you want to improve. Maybe you want to write better web copy or you want to market yourself better or have a better accounting system. Anything specific to your business will do. Once you have that one issue, go back to your list of funny things that have happened and spend another few minutes writing some stories, fleshing out the ones you already have or creating new ones.

Armed with the creativity from your humour exercises, take a look at your problem and start to brainstorm as many solutions as you can. Try to come up with really off-the-wall ideas, very serious ideas, and everything in between. It's possible that you will come up with the perfect idea early on, but what is more likely is that you will find the start of something. You may realise that you want to apply one of your ideas but don't know how yet. You might just have fun being a bit silly. That's all good.

The point is that even by coming up with silly ideas, you are teaching your mind to relax and think creatively about problems. Instead of seeing problems as obstacles, keeping humour close at hand helps you to see them as opportunities and sources of fun. Once you get used to seeing problems as sources of humour and chances for creativity, you actually begin to welcome them. It sounds strange, but it is true.

When it comes to seeing interpreting issues as a source of fun, I am really pleased to have been introduced to the work of freelance interpreter Matthew Perret. As well as having worked in the European institutions, he is also a stand-up comedian and one of the few people who can make *chuchotage* seem hilarious. Here is his interview for this chapter.

Interview with Matthew Perret

In your interview with Gala Gil Amat, you mentioned that you became an interpreter as a means of meeting people and using your languages while making money. How much did you really know about being an interpreter at that point?

I had read most of Seleskovitch as an undergrad, and met a conference interpreter who told me it was a malevolent world dominated by snobbish, competitive, intellectually mediocre show-offs, so I'd say I was pretty well prepared, and SCIC (the interpretation service of the European Commission) actually came as a pleasant surprise when I joined as a trainee.

I was performing on stage before I learnt any languages, and was very clear I was a touchy-feely people-person. I wanted to use my voice for a living, and just could not face the prospect of doing any written translation (other than literary). I still can't.

For the average person and even many clients, interpreting can seem a bit mystical and confusing. Have you found any ways to successfully explain to clients or the public what it is we do?

It's tricky. By definition, the people who need us most can never really understand what we do. They will need expert advice and a good deal of imagination in order to judge anything other than the 'end result'.

I also think we sometimes compound the problem – for instance, by describing the interpreter as a 'sort of translator'. People then expect us to reproduce a Power-Point's content regardless of speed of delivery, and so on. So I would tend to start by explaining that a carefully chosen group of communication professionals can remove the language barrier, and allow all participants an equal footing to play to their strengths, given the right conditions.

In some markets, such as the UK, multilingualism is barely understood as a con-cept. With such extreme cases, 'show, not tell' would be my motto. Maintain the highest standards, and influence decision-making professionals.

It's a balancing act: if we make it look too difficult, we are bad interpreters – we have drawn attention to the process, which gets in the way of communication. But if we make it look too easy, people might actually *think* it's easy, and hire us as some sort of afterthought after the coffee break and flowers have been arranged.

You have become slightly famous for being an interpreter and a stand-up comedi-an. How do you feel the two jobs relate?

Thank you for 'slightly famous'. That's now in print, so I shall be using it on my posters. It has a 'Dan Brown prose' feel to it too – you may not have heard of him, but I'm *telling you*, he's *slightly famous*.

Of course interpreters need to know languages, but to interpret a bee-keeper you have to be stung by a bee; to discuss science, law, economics, you need to be on top of those disciplines; to be the voice of a charismatic leader you need the gift of the gab yourself, and so on.

So anything from the *real world* that you can bring to interpreting is a plus: some of the best EU interpreters I know trained as lawyers or economists rather than primarily as linguists. I, like many others, have to do some swotting up on most subjects. What I bring to the party is an understanding of addressing an audience, handy for, er, motivational speakers and political extremists, for example.

One close similarity between the two lines of work is the cynicism of the off-stage/off-mic banter. We need a release valve.

And how do your managers and fellow interpreters react to you lampooning the everyday stresses of their work?

Lourdes de Rioja (A Word In Your Ear[8]) asked me to address issues that are a concern for beginners or students for her vlog (video blog). Since the resource has no formal status, I suggested a sketch format for some of them, as comedy seems to help get a message across. It appears to have helped start conversations about otherwise 'taboo' subjects such as 'impostor syndrome', burn-out, and mental health. Several colleagues have told me that when their partners complain that there's something wrong with them, they use my videos to explain exactly what that something is.

These shenanigans have led to a situation where interpreters, and indeed our bosses, do frequently point and laugh when they see me. I leave the reader to interpret that.

I know that some interpreters might find it difficult to see the funny side of our profession, given the pressures on the profession that we all know about. How would you advise them to mine their experience for humour?

I'm not sure I would describe it as a mining operation. At any rate: send a canary down first. Some people are apparently condemned to see life through the prism of comedy. If you are not, perhaps you can be liberated by glimpsing that absurdity, too.

It's not about whether something is valid, difficult, or even utterly sad and depressing – there are no 'funny' sides as opposed to 'unfunny' sides. A person desperately trying to take himself seriously is inherently hilarious. Not to single out the profession in any way, but I think many interpreters and indeed conference speakers are basically John Cleese trying to run a discreet, efficient hotel. What is there *not* to laugh at?

Are there any areas of interpreting that you would say are off limits to humour?

Like a true simultaneous interpreter, I couldn't help jumping ahead and answering that question before you asked it. No, I believe it is slightly absurd to claim that any aspect of human, or indeed animal or vegetable, life is 'off-limits' to an inquiring, questioning gaze. Comedy can be about sharing, or not sharing; it can be a benevolent or malevolent gaze. So ultimately I would say it's a transaction, like all communication – it takes two to tango and to make a joke 'funny'. Even a cruel parody of the most incompetent interpreter could potentially show what good interpreting means, and not at all devalue the profession. It all depends how it's done, and with whom you're making the transaction.

As in any other extracurricular activity, class clowns who go public must obviously respect professional confidentiality – they can't go blabbing about what colour shoes a head of state wears. (Truth is stranger than fiction, anyway.)

In this chapter, I cite studies that point to humour as helping to increase creativity. How do you think your sense of humour has helped your interpreting?

When it all goes horribly wrong, I laugh it off with a shrug and tell my boothmate a killer one-liner. It might not help my interpreting, but it certainly helps my blood pressure.

Lastly, if you met an interpreter who has the misfortune of wanting to become known for humour, what would you tell him or her?

You are really in the wrong profession. If you want to become known for your humour, go into accounting. There's less competition, and it will help you do your job better. My current accountant is German, slightly vague and incompetent, and very funny. His first words to me, down his bespectacled nose, were "So, Mr. Perret, what seems to be the trouble?" I still laugh about that.

Key chapter concepts

- Interpreting is funny.
- Humour, used well, seems to help us be more creative.
- Once you get used to seeing problems as sources of humour and chances for creativity, you actually begin to welcome them.
- We need a release valve.
- Many interpreters and indeed conference speakers are basically John Cleese trying to run a discreet, efficient hotel. What is there *not* to laugh at?

Putting it into practice

Questions to ask

How often do you find humour in your work?

How appropriate do you think it is to talk about the funny side of interpreting?

Actions to take

On your own

If you haven't already done so, do both of the exercises found earlier in this chapter. Note how you feel after writing all the challenges of your profession and how you feel after writing about funny situations. Which emotional state makes you feel more ready to face problems?

The next time you need to solve a problem and have some time to find a solution, start by taking ten to twenty minutes to think up some funny quips about interpreting. They could be silly puns, absurd comparisons, or strange questions and answers. Note the difference it makes to your problem solving.

If you can draw, think about starting a cartoon about the funny side of interpreting.

In a group

Invite some friends out to a café or pub and make a point of sharing funny interpreting stories.

If you are part of a group that has a newsletter or magazine, ask them to save some space for funny interpreting quips and stories.

Notes

1 No, that's not a typo. It really is a word in Scotland. I will leave it to readers to figure out what it means and what register it belongs to.
2 Josephine Chinying Lang and Chay Hoon Lee, 'Workplace Humor and Organizational Creativity', *The International Journal of Human Resource Management*, *21*, no. 1 (1 January 2010): 46–60. doi:10.1080/09585190903466855.
3 *Ibid.*, 55.
4 Alice M. Isen, Kimberly A. Daubman, and Gary P. Nowicki, 'Positive Affect Facilitates Creative Problem Solving', *Journal of Personality and Social Psychology*, *52*, no. 6 (1987): 1122.
5 Michele M. Tugade, Barbara L. Fredrickson, and Lisa Feldman Barrett, 'Psychological Resilience and Positive Emotional Granularity: Examining the Benefits of Positive Emotions on Coping and Health', *Journal of Personality*, *72*, no. 6 (December 2004): 1161–90. doi:10.1111/j.1467-6494.2004.00294.x.
6 www.specgram.com.
7 http://mrinterpreter.tumblr.com.
8 http://j.mp/WordInYourEar. (URL is case sensitive.)

Chapter 10

From adding value to adding clients

Chapter summary

This chapter covers:

* The reality of marketing to new clients,
* Where to go for help,
* Why interpreting will always have growth potential,
* The need to take ownership of our work.

We have seen the research. We have asked the big questions. Some of the more dedicated readers might have picked their way through the majority of the actions to take. Where do we go now?

Let's move away from our usual working environments and put ourselves in the place of a conference delegate. Imagine you are standing in the middle of an exhibition hall while thousands of people stream around you. Delegates from six continents rush from stand to stand, trying to make that deal, grab that customer, secure that important service.

You are there in the middle of that. Rather than being in the seminar room in a comfy booth or escorting high-level clients, you are a typical delegate. For the entirety of this day, you are in the same boat as everyone else – desperate to secure the kinds of business deals that will let you raise your rates and make you admired by your colleagues – one of whom is there with you. Marketing needs company, after all.

And what do you find? Many of those you meet on the stands give you something between a scowl and a pitying glare when you mention what you do.

"We already have translators," they say.

"You are in a hard business. Everyone already has their own team."

"Everywun here speekes Eenglish. We need no interprets."

Those are standard, and sometimes ironic, answers you might encounter. Some people are much nicer. When I had this experience, I gave away business cards and received promises of later contacts, amounting to a few doors ajar. Some doors might even be wide open in future.

Two notable conversations told me more than I could have learned from any research paper. One was a chat with the head of a start-up whose business strategy revolved around becoming a platform for other people to show off their excellence. I realised that my colleague and I were something of an anomaly.

"We don't get many interpreters here. I am not sure why. Your work is vital for everything we do."

In a marketplace that was literally crowded, we stood out by our mere presence. Even thinking that we belonged in the same physical space as our potential clients made us look like someone serious. If adding value is all about helping clients' events be successful, it will always be important to know what 'successful' actually means to your clients.

And then there was my first ever meeting with a high-end client, the kind every private-market interpreter dreams of working for. This client, whose history told me he had the money to pay, was very keen to know more about what interpreters do. Every area he works in is international. In his working environment, if one word goes wrong, the whole deal could collapse. He needed excellence and wanted to know where to find it.

For perhaps the first time in my career, I realised that clients are actually out there to be won. People still do have the money for interpreting and the desire for the best. It's just a matter of finding them.

Let's not kid ourselves. We can't afford to turn the realities of marketing, client acquisition, and networking into some kind of motivational talk. For those of us whose training included lots of material on international institutions and less on sales techniques, the learning curve can be steep. It only takes a few unsteady attempts to gain private clients to realise that the ability to bounce back from rejections is as necessary as the knack for creating pretty and useful term lists. We will hear 'no thank you' a lot before we get the first 'yes'.

Here again, the world of translation has gone there before us. Judy and Dagmar Jenner's book, *The Entrepreneurial Linguist*, alongside Marta Stelmaszak's *Business School for Translators*, gives the nuts and bolts that translators need in their business life. The *Starting Up as a Freelance Translator* course from the Institute of Translation and Interpreting lets translators learn with the help of experienced mentors. It wouldn't take too much creativity to apply the lessons from resources such as these to our work as interpreters.

If we are going to turn everything I have written on these pages into reality, we will need all the skills we have covered in the last nine chapters and more. The truth is that for many of us, the kinds of clients we want include people who have never seen an interpreter in the flesh. We can't expect clients to know or care about the merits of ISO booths, remote interpreting systems, detailed briefs, and the correct pronouns to use when working with interpreters. Some of them might not even know why they need to use professionals. Yet.

We may be the only people who are fully aware that our increasingly globalised world is going to need more interpreters, not fewer. Armed with a commitment to add value, dedication to professional development, commitment to professional

associations, healthy habits, a sense of humour, and everything else we have discussed, we will be perfectly positioned to meet that need. The rules of the game
are changing; it's up to us to change first.

What's in it for interpreters? I cannot honestly present you with any solid figures or empirical research. I don't know of any paper that tells us how much more
we can make if we change our perspective and work *with* clients instead of just
for them. All I can do is tell you the way it worked on one particular assignment.

Remember that truck job I mentioned in Chapter 9 – the one that involved being
ankle-deep in mud? The interpreting team did a great job – especially my boothmate who passed me her notes for the second iteration of a truck display. Over a
year after that job, I was feeling a bit down. I couldn't think of any example of a
time when my interpreting had made a difference. It seemed that all I did was go
into the booth, work, and go home. It was a bit depressing.

Since that truck job was the only one where I knew that the press from more
than one language were around, I did a bit of digging. Lo and behold, the French
industry press had published an article on precisely the kit displayed that day. Our
interpreting, as unconventional as the set-up might have been at times, led to a
favourable article for the end client.

I am not going to claim that it was all us – the trucks were impressive, the engi-
neers convincing, the directors inspiring. Yet I would argue that the interpreting
team, with their commitment to add value and help the event be successful, played
their part.

When we commit to adding value, it makes a difference. You see it in the number of clients who come back, the smiles on the faces of those present, the buzz in
the room, the improvement in patients, the fairness of the court case.

It might even make a difference to *us*. We all know about burn-out. We all
know how difficult and draining this job can be. What if we saw and understood
the difference we were making? What if our clients recognised our part in their
success? What if our rates were based not on standard agreements and grudging
acceptance but on the amount of impact we had on our clients?

We can but dream.

Whatever skills we have, there is plenty of space for us to use them. New companies are formed every day. New opportunities arise all the time. Our problem is
that we often think in terms of the big players, the big institutions, the sprawling
multinationals, the bilingual nations. Those big players are fine to court as clients,
but we can do more than just look to them for work. We can and should be offering
our skills to the dizzying variety of people and organisations who need them. We
can and should be seeing how our skills can open doors to other clients that might
have previously seemed shut.

That inspirational Deaf athlete might have an amazing story to tell, but he or
she may well need an interpreter to open up new audiences to hear it. That entrepreneur might have a wonderful idea, but without interpreters, they will be stuck
to those countries that speak their language. That lawyer might have sharp skills,
but without interpreters, their client list will be limited. There may well be a child

in the class who is an important scientist in the making, but the forces of migration may mean that he or she needs an interpreter to help with learning.

Every person who crosses a border, every company wanting to expand away from home, every speaker wanting to do a tour, every leader with a multilingual team, every teacher with a multilingual class – all will need us at some point. But they don't need the same version of us that is relevant to the staid board meeting or witness interview. They need someone who understands their individual needs and wants, who gets what their situation is all about and what it means to make their events work.

Why expand beyond our current horizons? George Leigh Mallory claimed he wanted to climb Mount Everest 'because it's there'. We should expand beyond our current territories simply because there are people there who need us or who will soon. We can never know how many of those people will be prepared to pay the rates we want until we ask.

What exactly am I proposing? I am proposing that we use our imaginations to look for clients far away from the confines of national contracts and ProZ project listings. What kind of client do you really want to work for? What would be your ideal assignment? Where do those people hang out? What do they look for in suppliers or work partners?

It is time to find all that out. It is time to care about the work our clients do, to take ownership of what comes out of our mouths or is created by our hands. If we are going to succeed outside the worlds we are used to, we need to not just think of ourselves as businesses but see our clients, even agencies, as valuable and worth the time and attention to nurture.

With that in mind, it is a real pleasure to give this last interview to Esther Navarro-Hall. She almost needs no introduction: respected interpreter trainer, inventor of a new interpreting mode, successful interpreter in her own right, she has nearly done it all in the world of interpreting. But what she is probably most famous for is her readiness to help others. She is the ideal person to ask for tips on breaking out of our current markets and into promising new ones. That is why this interview runs a little longer than the others.

Interview with Esther Navarro-Hall

You have a very varied career, covering university lecturing, interpreting, delivering courses for interpreters, and even inventing a new form of interpreting with various digital technologies, SimConsec™. How do you balance your own interpreting practice will all this?

I'm not sure I always accomplish the 'balance', but after thirty years in this business, interpreting is as exciting to me as ever. I find that I usually work in two different modes. The first mode is to take each day as it comes. I might be interpreting for a long stretch, with short breaks in between. Then I will barely have enough time to answer emails. If I'm working on an assignment that doesn't take up the whole day, I will devote more time to projects that demand my immediate attention. At this point in my career, I try to be more selective and accept assignments which allow me to learn the most, or are the best fit in terms of scheduling, economics, and subject matter.

Last year, I had the honour of being elected Chair of the National Association of Judiciary Interpreters and Translators (NAJIT). This poses additional challenges to that ever-elusive balance.

My training commitments have motivated me to work in a different way, hence, the second mode. A few years back I started to implement a plan which has worked quite well for me. I try to allocate a portion of my time each month to the four activities which are currently the most professionally significant for me: interpreting, teaching, consulting, and doing association/advocacy work. In order to work well in this mode, looking at the big picture is paramount.

Now, if I could just get a little more sleep, and a nice vacation in Maui with my husband, I'd be the happiest interpreter in the world.

Aside from your expertise in court interpreting, you also have experience in working in what some interpreters call the 'private market'. How did you gain these private clients?

After working for the big multinational organisations, I found that I enjoyed working in the private sector as well. It offered me a variety of work that kept me very interested and engaged. As I worked more in that vein, I realized that it also improved the breadth of my interpreting experience and provided me with some great thinking-on-my-feet skills.

I have been quite fortunate in that both the US market and the Mexican market lend themselves well to private enterprise. I decided back in 1993 that I craved the flexibility of freelancing. Thus, I shifted my focus from being an employee to having a B2B (business-to-business) approach. That way of doing business really appealed to me. It has also proven to be the key in building a solid client base. At first I didn't know that being an interpreter would require such a large dose of business acumen, so a lot of the strategies I have implemented in my business were learned 'in the field'.

I came upon my first big business opportunities via conference interpreting. Clients often look for a one-stop solution, and I was able to provide just that: interpreting, team coordination, and consulting, for example, or interpreting, training, and cultural information. Clients knew that they would receive high-quality services every time, so they didn't mind paying well for the full complement. Pretty soon, a happy client would recommend my services to another client, and so it went.

Although the legal, medical, and community interpreting fields are a bit more local, the same strategies apply. The point is to keep updating your suite of talents, whether it is interpreting skills, people skills, or entrepreneurial skills. As the years go by, you'll start to amass a wealth of information, practical skills, and relevant ideas. Discerning clients will be more than willing to invest in those services, individually or as a package. When you work in this fashion, your field of choice does not matter.

For many years, interpreter training has been dominated by preparing interpreters for work in courts, diplomacy, and medicine. What specialist skills might private-market interpreters need?

I can organize the skills that come to mind in two different categories: business skills and what I call the 'intangibles of interpreting'. When I was getting ready to strike out on my own, I was sorely lacking in marketing, financial planning, and negotiating skills, just to name a few. In fact, I was self-taught in most of these crucial business skills. I read, attended workshops, and talked to entrepreneurs in other professions. I tell you, there is no incentive like living from paycheck to paycheck as a freelancer. You soon learn that if you are to succeed in this profession, not only as creative artist but also as an effective entrepreneur, you have to let go of the things that don't work, *very* quickly. You also need to set goals and objectives that keep propelling you forward.

Some of the 'intangible skills' that I try to instil in my students, and are often not taught in 'interpreting school', are: a spirit of cooperation, camaraderie, and sharing; a mentality of openness and flexibility; a way of working with your inner voice; and a vision of expansiveness and creativity in interpreting, among many others. Whether in the booth, at the witness stand, or in the OR, one of the most important things I have learned in the private market is how to change gears quickly, diplomatically, and with efficiency.

I employ a holistic approach to interpreter training because I strongly believe that these skills can be taught at the same time as the technical skills you have mentioned. We might need to revise our training-of-trainers curricula, and our own curricula as trainers, in order to pass this on to future generations.

I could also devote a whole chapter to the technology skills which are currently expected of interpreters in the field and are not being taught in most training or interpreting schools, but I am hopeful that this will also change soon.

Some interpreters may feel daunted by the private market, as it involves learning about business-to-business selling and dealing with corporate decision makers. What have you learned about navigating these challenges?

I come from a position of 'What can I provide for my clients that they have not considered in their search?' or 'What unknowns can I illuminate as they make their decision?' Many times, prospective clients do not have a clear picture of what to expect, so I guide them through the whole interpreting process. Navigating these waters can be challenging, but knowing that we are the cornerstone to communication between companies, cultures, societies, institutions, or individuals, we need to learn to negotiate from a position of power.

One small personal example: years ago, I started requesting payment with a fifteen-day net from my clients, or immediately after services were provided. Some of my fellow interpreters assured me that this would never happen. Both direct clients and agencies started to work with me in that respect. It is now common practice for 90 per cent of my clients – and submitting payment online is also becoming more the rule than the exception.

The main themes of this book are adding value to our clients and adding value to our profession. What can we do to help private and corporate clients see us as people who add value to them?

The first thing we need to understand is the importance of what we do. Then we need to ask ourselves what we are doing in our own practice to become better at what we do – in all aspects. The rest will follow. If a portion of our own practice is not working, we need to do some troubleshooting. Is it because we need to create a business presence that is easily accessible to everyone? Is it because once we have created a relationship of trust with our client, we are doing very little to retain them as a client or to make them aware of additional services? Is it because we have built a solid practice but we are not interested in collaborating with our colleagues or innovating? We should ask ourselves these questions often. Interpreting is a dynamic business, so we need to keep pace with our market in order to obtain the visibility we need.

Sometimes I feel we spend a lot of time trying to convince an 'audience' of our value, when we are the ones who need convincing. We often talk about the low pay many clients expect us to accept for our services, or decry the lack of respect towards our profession. Nevertheless, clients are smart enough to know that if an interpreter lowers his price so he can get the job, he will probably sell his services to the lowest bidder. In essence, we are telling clients how to treat us by the way we treat our profession; but the old adage 'you get what you pay for' is something we all believe. However, I believe that more important than the concern about what other interpreters are charging is what we can do in our own practice to create a market which works for us. In order to do this, we need to present a perfect solution for each client – something we are more than qualified to do. Then we need to inform them how much they will be paying for our services.

Could you give an example of how you added value during a private-market assignment?

I have many examples I could provide, but, recently, I was interpreting for a well-known politician and he asked me something about my culture in the middle of an interpretation. I answered his question, he added something quickly to his speech, and, as a result, he was a big hit. His audience realized that he was interested in them. They found that characteristic very appealing, and communication went swimmingly after that.

How far do you think our current professional ethics, standards, and working methods work in the private market? What might we need to change or improve to add more value to such clients?

I believe that as a profession we need to work on establishing additional standards, best practices, and work on revising our ethics where needed. We also need to work on securing funding to train interpreters so they can stay on top of their game the way other professions do. If we train and prepare diligently, we will become even more visible in the community of professionals. There is no other profession in this world like ours, and there are not many of us to begin with, but continuing interpreter education requirements could teach interpreters what they may not know and add more of the value we spoke about before.

I also think we need to start a bit earlier. I often tell my colleagues that I would love to hear children say in the near future, 'When I grow up, I want to be an interpreter', just like they aspire to be a fireman or an astronaut.

Lastly, if you were to give one piece of advice to interpreters aspiring to work in the private market, what would you say?

It is difficult for me to limit this to one piece of advice, so here it goes: the private market demands a wide range of skills that are often overlooked during training. Make sure that you procure these skills for yourself, but always work with your colleagues in the process. Get involved in organisations that can have a positive effect on the profession and always stay well informed on the latest developments. Interpreting is a tremendous learning experience, but it will not make for a prosperous business and it will not be of great importance, unless you infuse it with love and caring. Respect the profession and your fellow interpreters. Love our profession enough to do your part to move it forward through education, preparation, and the highest possible standards.

Key chapter concepts

- In a marketplace that was literally crowded, we stood out by our mere presence.
- People still do have the money for interpreting and the desire for the best. It's just a matter of finding them.
- Whatever skills we have, there is plenty of space for us to use them.
- We need to learn to negotiate from a position of power.
- We need to present a perfect solution for each client.

Putting it into practice

Questions to ask

What does your ideal client look like?

How can you find your ideal client?

What are the factors that seem to stop you from expanding your current list of clients?

What can you do to eliminate or reduce those factors?

What is your next step?

Actions to take

On your own

Go back to the Questions to Ask section and write down as much detail as you can for each. Make a plan to meet one new potential client this month.

In a group

Find a group of two or three other interpreters who work in the same setting, but not necessarily the same languages as you, and attend a trade event together. Talk to clients both individually and as a small group and share your findings and successes together.

Inventing the future

Today, professional interpreters stand at a crossroads. Behind them, the well-worn paths to professionalism and even regular work seem to be showing signs of wear and tear. I wrote those words in the Introduction and they are worth repeating here. If you have read this far through the book, you have read all about the real challenges we face and the real potential we all have. Interpreting is not dead; in fact, it is very much alive and vibrant. Its continued health, however, is in our hands. No client, no matter how powerful, can force interpreting into recession. No agreement, no matter how unfair, can spell the end of our profession. The people responsible for the future of interpreting are professional interpreters, and it will always be that way.

If that seems daunting, it is just because we are not used to thinking in those terms. We have rarely dared to think that we are the people who can make a difference. We are the people whose decisions will change interpreting for the better or the worse. If there is one message that I want people to get from this book, it's that as we add value to our clients and our profession, we make a difference, not only to those for whom we work but to our entire industry. Assignment by assignment, client by client, association by association, excellence and commitment get noticed and help to shape the future.

On this very subject, while I was finishing the early draft of this book, Alexander Drechsel, a staff interpreter for European institutions, released an excellent blog post called Disruption in Interpreting: It's History Repeating[1]. His argument was that interpreting has always been shaped and strengthened by change: from the technological feat of creating simultaneous interpreting for the early international organisations to the modern changes brought about by the ever-presence of the internet.

His conclusions are remarkably similar to mine, if couched in different language. Yes, human interpreters will always be needed, he argues, but the services we offer and how we offer them will need to change. Instead of being knocked down by technological and market changes, he argued that we need to master them and even turn them to our own advantage. In other words, we need to think creatively about the challenges we face, which in turn will add value to our clients.

That two interpreters with such different backgrounds and such different clients should come to such similar conclusions should be no surprise. As Alexander points out, the facts are there for all to see. All we need to do is be brave enough to accept them and make sense of them.

This book has been all about doing just that. Instead of allowing technological and market changes to cripple us in hopelessness, I hope that this book has given you the insights and tools to see opportunities in the obstacles and potential in the problems.

I know enough about interpreters to imagine that a large proportion of those who read this book have skipped the questions and actions and blown right through to this point. I would also hazard a guess that some of those who have done that feel that they might have learned something but are a bit stuck for how to put it into practice. To them, as a fellow book-skipper, I have this to say: slow down, take a breath, and work things out slowly.

I firmly believe that we have only really learned something when we attempt, even haltingly at first, to put it into practice. That's what I am going to do. Even as the person who wrote this, I have to admit that I still need to learn to put it into practice in my own work. So let's do this together. Pick one chapter for one month and work through all the exercises, taking a maximum of one a week. With the questions, take time to really think about your answers and, just like I said in the Introduction, think about what your answers say about you as an interpreter. Are you happy with what you see? If not, fear not; just keep going and keep improving.

If I were to start anywhere, it would be Chapter 1. We can't go wrong committing ourselves to adding value to our clients. After that, I need to work on my fitness and form a CPD plan. What will it be for you? Write down the chapter you are concentrating on for the first month and put that note somewhere prominent.

Let's take the journey together to build a profession that becomes renowned for adding value and committing to excellence. As computer expert Alan Kay said, "The best way to predict the future is to invent it". It's time for interpreters to become inventors. Let's go.

Note

1 www.adrechsel.de/dolmetschblog/disruption.

Bibliography

Angelelli, Claudia. *Revisiting the Interpreter's Role: A Study of Conference, Court, and Medical Interpreters in Canada, Mexico, and the United States. Vol. 55*. Amsterdam: John Benjamins Publishing Company, 2004.

Beaton, Morven. 'Interpreted Ideologies in Institutional Discourse: The Case of the European Parliament'. *The Translator, 13*, no. 2 (2007): 271–96.

Beaton-Thome, Morven. 'Negotiating Identities in the European Parliament: The Role of Simultaneous Interpreting', in *Text and Context: Essays on Translation and Interpreting in Honour of Ian Mason*, Manchester: St. Jerome, 2010, 117–38.

Benton, David, Marie-Pierre Ruffin, Taous Lassel, Samantha Nabb, Michaël Messaoudi, Sophie Vinoy, Didier Desor, and Vincent Lang. 'The Delivery Rate of Dietary Carbohydrates Affects Cognitive Performance in Both Rats and Humans'. *Psychopharmacology, 166*, no. 1 (2003): 86–90.

Berk-Seligson, Susan. *The Bilingual Courtroom: Court Interpreters in the Judicial Process*. Chicago: University of Chicago Press, 2002.

Cambridge, Jan. 'Public Service Interpreting: Practice and Scope for Research', in *Translation Research and Interpreting Research: Traditions, Gaps and Synergies*, edited by Christina Schäffner, 2004, 49–51.

Chang, Yu-Kai, J. D. Labban, J. I. Gapin, and J. L. Etnier. 'The Effects of Acute Exercise on Cognitive Performance: A Meta-Analysis'. *Brain Research*, no. 1453 (2012): 87–101.

Clifford, Andrew. 'Is Fidelity Ethical?. The Social Role of the Healthcare Interpreter'. *TTR: Traduction, Terminologie, Rédaction, 17*, no. 2 (2004). www.erudit.org/revue/ttr/2004/v17/n2/013273ar.html.

Colcombe, Stanley, and Arthur F. Kramer. 'Fitness Effects on the Cognitive Function of Older Adults: A Meta-Analytic Study'. *Psychological Science, 14*, no. 2 (2003): 125–30.

Cummins, Ann. 'Clinical Supervision: The Way Forward? A Review of the Literature'. *Nurse Education in Practice, 9*, no. 3 (2009): 215–20.

Dean, Robyn K. 'Condemned to Repetition? An Analysis of Problem-Setting and Problem-Solving in Sign Language Interpreting Ethics'. *Translation & Interpreting, 6*, no. 1 (2014): 60–75.

Dean, Robyn K., and Robert Q. Pollard Jr. 'Beyond "Interesting": Using Demand Control Schema to Structure Experiential Learning', in *In Our Hands: Educating Healthcare Interpreters*, edited by K. Malcolm and Laurie Swabey, 77–104. Washington, DC: Gallaudet University Press, 2012.

Diriker, Ebru. *De-/Re-Contextualizing Conference Interpreting: Interpreters in the Ivory*

Tower?, Vol. 53. Amsterdam: John Benjamins Publishing Company, 2004.

Djovčoš, Martin, and Zuzana Djovčošova. 'Aphasia and Interpreting: Aphasia-Based Interpreting Exercises'. *FORUM*, *11*, no. 1 (2013): 23–49.

Downie, Jonathan. 'What Every Client Wants?(Re) Mapping the Trajectory of Client Expectations Research'. *Meta: Journal Des traducteurs/ Meta: Translators' Journal*, *60*, no. 1 (2015): 18–35.

Eraslan, Seyda. '"Cultural Mediator" or "Scrupulous Translator"? Revisiting Role, Context, and Culture in Consecutive Conference Interpreting'. Edited by Pieter Boulogne. Translation and Its Others. Selected Papers of the CETRA Research Seminar in Translation Studies 2007, 2008.

———. 'International Knowledge Transfer in Turkey: The Consecutive Interpreter's Role in Context'. Unpublished Doctoral Thesis, Rovira i Virgili University, 2011.

Ericsson, K. Anders, Neil Charness, Paul J. Feltovich, and Robert R. Hoffman. *The Cambridge Handbook of Expertise and Expert Performance*. Cambridge University Press, 2006.

Gile, Daniel. *Basic Concepts and Models for Interpreter and Translator Training*, Vol. 8. Amsterdam: John Benjamins Publishing Company, 2009.

———. 'Testing the Effort Models: Tightrope Hypothesis in Simultaneous Interpreting-A Contribution'. *Hermes*, *23*, no. 1999 (1999): 153–72.

———. 'Translation Research versus Interpreting Research: Kinship, Differences, and Prospects for Partnership', in *Translation Research and Interpreting Research: Traditions, Gaps and Synergies*, edited by Christina Schäffner, 10–34, 2004.

Hermann, Alfred. 'Interpreting in Antiquity', in *The Interpreting Studies Reader*, edited by Franz Pochhacker and Miriam Shlesinger, translated by Ruth Morris, 15–22. London: Routledge, 1956.

Isen, Alice M., Kimberly A. Daubman, and Gary P. Nowicki. 'Positive Affect Facilitates Creative Problem Solving.' *Journal of Personality and Social Psychology*, *52*, no. 6 (1987): 1122.

Kurz, Ingrid. 'Conference Interpreting: Quality in the Ears of the User'. *Meta*, *46*, no. 2 (2001): 394–409.

Lang, Josephine Chinying, and Chay Hoon Lee. 'Workplace Humor and Organizational Creativity'. *The International Journal of Human Resource Management*, *21*, no. 1 (1 January 2010): 46–60. doi:10.1080/09585190903466855.

Mack, Gabriela, and Lorella Cattaruzza. 'User Surveys in SI: A Means of Learning about Quality and/or Raising Some Reasonable Doubts', in *Topics in Interpreting Research*, edited by Jorma Tommola, 37–51. Turku: University of Turku, Centre for Translation and Interpreting, 1995.

Ozolins, Uldis. 'Telephone Interpreting: Understanding Practice and Identifying Research Needs'. *Translation & Interpreting*, *3*, no. 2 (27 February 2012): 33–47. doi:10.12807/t&i. v3i2.136.

Pöchhacker, Franz. 'Conference Interpreting: Surveying the Profession'. *Translation and Interpreting Studies*, *4*, no. 2 (2009): 172–86. doi:10.1075/tis.4.2.02poc.

Pym, Anthony. 'Training Translators', in *Oxford Handbook Translation Studies*, edited by Kirsten Malmkjaer and Kevin Windle, 475–89. Oxford, United Kingdom: Oxford University Press, 2011. Retrieved from www.researchgate.net/profile/Anthony_Pym2/ publication/242711915_Translator_training/links/53fd94050cf2dca8000353cf.pdf.

————. 'Translator Associations—from Gatekeepers to Communities'. *Target*, *26*, no. 3 (2014): 466–91.

Rosenberg, Ellen, Yvan Leanza, and Robbyn Seller. 'Doctor–Patient Communication in Primary Care with an Interpreter: Physician Perceptions of Professional and Family Interpreters'. *Patient Education and Counseling*, *67*, no. 3 (2007): 286–92.

Spencer, Jeremy PE. 'Food for Thought: The Role of Dietary Flavonoids in Enhancing Human Memory, Learning and Neuro-Cognitive Performance'. *Proceedings of the Nutrition Society*, *67*, no. 2 (2008): 238–52.

Tiselius, Elisabet. 'Experience and Expertise in Conference Interpreting: An Investigation of Swedish Conference Interpreters'. University of Bergen, 2012.

————. 'Peak Performance for Interpreters: Practice Right'. eCPD Webinars. Retrieved from www.ecpdwebinars.co.uk/downloads/performance-for-interpreters.

Torres Díaz, María Gracia, and Alessandro Ghignoli. 'Interpreting Performed by Professionals of Other Fields: The Case of Sports Commentators'. Gemersheim, Germany, 2014. Retrieved from http://dspace.uma.es/xmlui/handle/10630/8130.

Tugade, Michele M., Barbara L. Fredrickson, and Lisa Feldman Barrett. 'Psychological Resilience and Positive Emotional Granularity: Examining the Benefits of Positive Emotions on Coping and Health'. *Journal of Personality*, *72*, no. 6 (December 2004): 1161–90. doi:10.1111/j.1467-6494.2004.00294.x.

Turner, Graham H. 'Towards Real Interpreting', in *Sign Language Interpreting and Interpreter Education: Directions for Research and Practice*, edited by M. Marschark, R. Peterson, and E. Winston, 253–65. New York: Oxford University Press, 2005.

Turner, Graham H., and Frank Harrington. 'Issues of Power and Method in Interpreting Research', in *Intercultural Faultlines: Research Models in Translation Studies*, edited by Maeve Olohan, 253–65. Research Models in Translation Studies 1. Manchester: St Jerome Publishing, 2000.

VandeWalle, Don, Steven P. Brown, William L. Cron, and John W. Slocum Jr. 'The Influence of Goal Orientation and Self-Regulation Tactics on Sales Performance: A Longitudinal Field Test.' *Journal of Applied Psychology*, *84*, no. 2 (1999): 249.

Wenger, Etienne. 'Communities of Practice: A Brief Introduction', 2011. Retrieved from https://scholarsbank.uoregon.edu/xmlui/handle/1794/11736.

Zwischenberger, Cornelia. 'Simultaneous Conference Interpreting and a Supernorm that Governs It All'. *Meta: Journal Des traducteurs/ Meta: Translators' Journal*, *60*, no. 1 (2015): 90–111.

Index

Made in the USA
Middletown, DE
19 January 2025

69821247R00071